Before We Begin, A Bit About You

Hi. Good to see you've got this book in your hand and reading this page. The thing is, I know nothing about you – and I have no idea what's brought you to this moment where you are standing (Sitting? Lying?) here reading this page. I didn't do any market research, I didn't ask anyone if they wanted a book like this, I didn't even have a 'target market' in mind when I wrote it.

When publishing a book the publisher will always ask the hopeful author 'Who's the target market?'. I'm not sure what I said, but I know I lied as to the audience for this book and the motivations for buying it. You might be someone in the market research industry outraged by the title; you may be a small business owner wanting to know how to build a brand centric business; you could be a marketer or a CEO empathising with the title; or you could be my wife, Anna, supporting me. Or you might be someone completely different.

I didn't listen to the customer (possibly you) when I wrote this book, but the fact you are reading this is just the smallest evidence point to suggest I was right about not doing so.

Anyway, enough with the smug, circular arguments, I hope you enjoy *Stop Listening to the Customer: Try hearing your brand instead* – whoever you are.

Adam Ferrier

STOP
LISTENING
TO THE
CUSTOMER

STOP LISTENING TO THE CUSTOMER

...TRY HEARING YOUR BRAND INSTEAD

Adam Ferrier
with Jen Flemming

WILEY

First published in 2020 by John Wiley & Sons Australia, Ltd
42 McDougall St, Milton Qld 4064

Office also in Melbourne

Typeset in Warnock Pro Regular 11pt/15pt

© John Wiley & Sons Australia, Ltd 2020

The moral rights of the authors have been asserted

ISBN: 978-0-730-37057-4

A catalogue record for this book is available from the National Library of Australia

Cover design by Ben Couzens

Cover photo by Marcus Byrne

Photos on pages 61 to 62 © XiXinXing / Shutterstock;
© Deflector Image / Shutterstock;
© sebra / Shutterstock

Printed in Singapore by Markono Print Media Pte Ltd

10 9 8 7 6 5 4 3 2 1

Disclaimer
The material in this publication is of the nature of general comment only, and does not represent professional advice. It is not intended to provide specific guidance for particular circumstances and it should not be relied on as the basis for any decision to take action or not take action on any matter which it covers. Readers should obtain professional advice where appropriate, before making any such decision. To the maximum extent permitted by law, the authors and publisher disclaim all responsibility and liability to any person, arising directly or indirectly from any person taking or not taking action based on the information in this publication.

contents

dedications and thanks

This book is dedicated to Anna, Asterix and Arturo. Thank you for everything. You're my number one. Anna, I'm sorry. I should have listened to you and bought a grate for the fireplace. The hole in the floorboards caused by the flying bit of wood could have been avoided if I had just heard you. Asterix, I'm also sorry for not listening to you. That same hole could have been avoided if I'd raised my head when you warned me there was smoke coming from the floor. I'll do my best to look up next time.

On another note, I want to thank my business partners, everyone I work with at Thinkerbell and our clients. In two short years, you've given me so many great ideas to write about.

Thanks to the incredible team at Wiley, especially Lucy Raymond for liking the idea of 'Hey big nose' and helping make this project happen. To the brilliant and sensitive editor, Allison Hiew. To the hardcore cognitively ambidextrous Chris Shorten, thanks for pulling the whole thing together. To my co-writer Jen Fleming, who is beyond skilled at deciphering 'Ferrier'. This book would have been twice as long if you hadn't chopped my words.

preface
getting from awkward to awesome

My parents sent me to a prestigious private school in Perth called Scotch College, which is the type of school attended by today's leaders of tomorrow and where boys become men. I never saw myself as one of tomorrow's leaders. Here's a story that sums up my school experience. (Brace yourself: it's a good one.)

My mother (oh god, I'm already talking about Mum and I haven't even started the book) had what can only be described as a laissez-faire approach to parenting. I was pretty much a free-range kid with very few boundaries. I didn't wear shoes and never changed my clothes. I'd wear the same outfit for weeks on end. Yes, I slept, went to school, slept, went to school in the same clothes. Bath night was the first night of the month. 'Kids don't get dirty,' my mum would say, even as my skin became progressively darker as the month went on. When I came home from school, I ate cereal or a big bowl of defrosted frozen peas. I didn't do any homework. During my years at primary school, I was always in trouble because I did my own thing. My parents loved me, but my home life was somewhat unconventional. (If you're wondering why such laidback parents sent me to Scotch, my theory is it came down to the 'price placebo effect' – the more you pay, the better you think it will be.)

Scotch College had a uniform, including a tie and shoes. Socks had to be pulled up, shirt tucked in, all of that. None of which worked for me. My uniform was a hand-me-down with buttons missing, my shirt was always out, and my tie would never do up properly. I looked incredibly dishevelled, which accurately reflected my attitude at school. I was the classic rebel without a cause, constantly in trouble and always at odds with the teachers and other students. I was smart enough, but my grades suffered — considerably.

Even though I loved sport and drama, I wasn't very good at either. If you did drama classes at Scotch, you were committing yourself to years of bullying hell. Asthma made me a poor runner. A lack of self-discipline meant I couldn't stick at anything. In year 10 I made the tennis team but was kicked off for fighting with another team member.

You should be getting a picture of someone who was not at their best at school. Throughout this tumultuous period in my life, most of the teachers were blasé about my performance. Thirty other kids in the class needed attention. I don't think the teachers enjoyed watching my pain, but they were certainly indifferent. And then, after five years of this mayhem (in my mind), something odd and rather cruel happened. It was the last day of school — muck-up day.

For the final assembly, all 140 boys in our house squashed into a crowded science lab — that's 140 boys sitting, standing, sweating — a coliseum of testosterone. The housemaster was a nice enough guy, a well-known former squash champion and diligent teacher. I always found him to be reasonable, and the other students loved him. He was very athletic and sported a thick, macho moustache. On this last day of school, for reasons I'll never know, he began the final homeroom meeting by saying, 'Adam Ferrier, could you please come down here and stand next to me?' As I made my way to the front of the class, I wondered if I'd done something worthy of merit. When I got to the front of the room, he ushered me to stand right next to him. He then placed one hand on my shoulder and in front of a silent room, he said, 'Everyone look at Adam Ferrier. Don't forget him. Adam is the perfect example of someone whose parents have wasted their money sending their son to a school like Scotch.'

Standing there, no doubt with my shirt hanging out and socks down, I felt embarrassed and confused — although I'm sure I managed to put a stupid smirk on my face. I don't remember if the other boys laughed at this; after his opening remarks, the rest was a bit of a blur. Perhaps they were just as shocked as I was at the teacher's brutality. Why did he do this? Maybe he was using me to motivate the other boys. It hurt because it was clear he assumed I was completely useless. He thought that because I didn't fit in with the school system I had wasted my opportunities, and that, because I didn't conform and demonstrate my leadership potential, my parents had wasted their money.

Although I didn't enjoy high school one bit, it solidified my character and conviction. I distrust authority and structure, and value forging my own path. These values are neither good nor bad, right nor wrong. But they sit nicely with me. My parents didn't waste their money sending me to Scotch; not fitting in was, and remains, my virtue. It just took time for me to realise this.

Fast forward to many years after finishing school. By now, I've achieved some success in advertising. I've won awards and recognition, and regularly speak at conferences and in the media — becoming (some might say) an industry expert. I'm also happily married to a wonderful woman, Anna, and we have two amazing boys, Asterix and Arturo. So, you could say in some respects I've got my shit together. Recently, I was the keynote speaker at an advertising conference, and my presentation went well. The following day I received an email in my inbox that read:

Hi Adam,

I was at the talk last night and what you said really touched me. You are obviously a really awkward guy but have somehow turned awkward into awesome.

As a somewhat awkward art director myself, I'm wondering what advice you might have for me and my career in advertising?

I love this email. It was an external validation of something I worked out years ago. My housemaster was wrong. Sure, I didn't fit in and couldn't be contained. But I didn't waste my opportunities at Scotch. I'm still dishevelled, and I still have terrible organisational and management skills. But I've done my own thing, trodden my scrappy path and, as that lovely chap put it, turned awkward into awesome (if not humble!).

What's the usual advice to outsiders? Fit in and conform. Be like everyone else. This is terrible advice for people and, as I'll argue in this book, terrible advice for brands too. Unfortunately, the more opinions we gather, the more voices we listen to, the stronger the inexorable force drawing us towards mediocrity and away from what makes us unique. There is an alternative. In addition to accepting who you are, I reckon you should dial up your difference and your distinctiveness.

Allow me to switch our focus now to brands and business. For some time now, there's been an obsession with asking the customer what they want. In my view, customers shouldn't be your driving force. Instead, you should focus on defining a clearly articulated brand that sets you apart. If you listen to the customer, the brand will become like other brands. Generic.

I've always prided myself on holding different and unconventional ideas. However, it's difficult to swim against the strong currents of conformity. At its heart, this book makes a case for ignoring others' opinions and following your path.

Adam Ferrier
January 2020

introduction

If a good brand is a promise, then a great brand is a promise kept. I don't know who came up with this saying. Many moons ago, I quoted it during a workshop and it kind of stuck. But I stole it from someone else, and the internet attributes the phrase to many. Either way, I like it, and it works. A brand signifies to a consumer that the good or service they are looking for is available. Inherent in a brand is a promise to deliver a set of values or benefits. The more a brand delivers on its promise, the stronger that brand becomes.

Brand valuation estimates the financial value of the brand. Companies such as Interbrand, Brand Finance and Kantar specialise in measuring the economic contribution a brand makes to a business. According to Kantar, the top 100 global brands had a combined value of US$4.7 trillion in 2019.[1] The top 10 brands were Apple, Amazon, Google, Microsoft, Visa, Facebook, Alibaba, Tencent, McDonald's and AT&T. Many argue that the brand is the most critical part of a company and that divorcing the brand from the company is futile because, if done well, the brand *is* the company.

Seth Godin is a US marketing expert who summarises brand value in this way:

A brand's value is merely the sum total of how much extra people will pay, or how often they choose, the expectations, memories, stories and relationships of one brand over the alternatives.

It's not the supply chain, staff, marketing, machines or capital expenditure, networks or the things they make. The value — the thing that people pay for — is called 'brand equity'. This is the value people ascribe to the brand over and above an unbranded copycat alternative. 'Brand value' is an inward-looking term, meaning the value the organisation puts on the brand. If you're an old-school accountant (and I can't imagine there are many reading this book), brand value roughly translates as 'goodwill', the intangible value in a company that permeates everything it does. If that argument doesn't cut it for you, try iconic punk songwriter and performer Patti Smith's take on it. In a short sentence she distills the difference in value from what one does (music), to asking the big question: 'Rock and roll is dream soup. What's your brand?'

But my intention isn't to convince you about the value of brands. I'm imagining you've come to this book knowing a bit about marketing and branding. Instead, I want to explore how businesses inadvertently devalue brands and make them generic. It's a significant issue in the world of marketing at the moment. If you own a company, business or brand or have a degree of influence over a brand, then look at what you can do to maintain a robust, distinctive and ultimately valuable brand. You see, the world of branding has become a little screwed up. When a business isn't clear about its brand, it risks becoming generic and leaving money on the table. I believe the main reason businesses are doing this is because they're listening to the one person they shouldn't. The customer.

Years ago, I worked at the legendary advertising agency Saatchi & Saatchi (the only advertising agency your parents have heard of) and Old El Paso was one of my first accounts. In a nice twist of fate, I'm working with the brand again. When Saatchi signed on, the team had a three-day induction with Old El Paso's parent company, General Mills. At the end of the first day, we watched a video that showcased the wonderful achievements of General Mills during its century of operation. I haven't forgotten the dramatic voice-over at the end of the video proclaiming something to the effect of 'the company's brand is now in your hands, so please don't stuff it up'. I loved the honesty of this corporate video despite the abrupt ending. My take-home message was that brands can't just tick along on their own. They need to be managed, and, if poorly managed, they'll die.

A brand is both valuable and sensitive. It's difficult and expensive to create a brand that stands for something in a consumer's mind. This understates the challenge. Many elements need to go right to create a brand that's motivating, credible and differentiated. It needs to create strong associations, be salient and leave the impression that the brand will help satisfy wants and needs. In prioritising the customer, and taking a customer-led approach, I worry it's at the expense of brand-led thinking. And it's making brands less robust. This book will reveal why brands are becoming weaker and less valuable and how marketers are losing their nerve. It's not all doom and gloom with advice and suggestions for how to build strong brands.

This book includes interviews with industry leaders, research from marketing sciences, anecdotes from my life as a psychologist and advertiser and a fair whack of pure opinion. I've thrown each of these ingredients into a mixing bowl, given them a stir, baked them in the oven and plated up. I hope the result is a tasty, satisfying dish.

Apparently on the outside of a building of the University of Chicago is a plaque that reads, 'Within these walls contain no wisdom. Only the ability to weigh and consider'. Whether or not this plaque actually exists, the message applies to these pages as well. I've structured the book as follows:

The Background:

♦ **Chapter 1:** 'Stop the consumer obsession' explores the proposition that we are consumer-led and not brand-led. It suggests this is the fundamental issue facing business today.

The Issue:

♦ **Chapter 2:** 'Consumers lie' outlines the dangers of putting the consumer first. Consumers can't be believed and are unreliable witnesses of their own behaviour, and even worse predictors of their future behaviour.

- **Chapter 3:** 'Listening to the consumer eliminates value' discusses the fundamental issue with listening to the consumer: it eliminates value from your business. The more you listen to consumers, the less valuable your business becomes.

- **Chapter 4:** 'Listening to the consumer makes your business homogeneous' argues you not only eliminate value, but your brand will start looking like the others. Homogeneity in brands is a significant issue, with people finding it difficult to distinguish one brand from another. The more a company listens to consumers, the worse this becomes.

The Hope:

- **Chapter 5:** 'They who hear their brand' outlines how brands that don't listen to the consumer are the most successful. It also goes beyond consumer brands to look at the arts and political polling. The less we listen to consumers, the stronger companies become.

The Solution:

- **Chapter 6:** 'Create the category' encourages marketers to make a brand that operates in an entirely new space. This is hard to do, but invaluable. If a marketer can create this, that's great. If not, chapters 7 to 10 may help.

- **Chapter 7:** 'Define the brand' looks at my business's formula for brand-building, BXB4CX.

- **Chapter 8:** 'Gonzo marketing 1: Fire the CEO' looks at the ideal organisational structure to be brand-led in your thinking. Spoiler alert: if the CEO doesn't get it, it's going to be an uphill battle. Another spoiler alert: if your company has a marketing department, you might be in trouble too.

- **Chapter 9:** 'Gonzo marketing 2: Put the customer second' looks at the roll-out of a brand to ensure everyone understands it from the inside out.

- **Chapters 10 and 11** examine two themes that never emerge in consumer research. Both explore the positives of the negative, or the strengths in weakness. Chapter 10: 'Embracing the negative' explains how to embrace negative ideas strategically, while chapter 11: 'Creating weakness' offers practical suggestions to make consumers pay attention through friction, mistakes and waste.

♦ **Chapter 12:** 'Ask what the consumer can do for you' suggests you stop asking what you can do for the consumer and ask what they can do for you. This is the kind of thing you won't discover in a focus group.

A Final Word:

♦ **Chapter 13:** 'The closing argument' is a brief recap.

Experts I've spoken to or exchanged emails with include Australian tennis legend John Newcombe; celebrity turned technology entrepreneur Jules Lund; vice chair of Ogilvy, Rory Sutherland; Australia's current number one chief marketing officer, Lisa Ronson; marketing sciences sensei Wiemer Snijders; and founder of pleasure business OMGyes, Rob Perkins. To you, and others who appear throughout this book, thank you for your time and insights.

A confession

You might think it's slightly worrying that this book is by someone who's built a career on consumer insights and used those insights to inform strategy. I've insisted my companies have research capabilities, including a focus group room within the agency, and my current company, Thinkerbell, is no exception. The room has ultra-high-fidelity sound and a one-way mirror. However, the name of the insights and research business is 'Hocus Focus' — a nod to the fact that even though research purports to be the truth, it's often a sleight of hand or just plain wrong. Research can be useless and, in the wrong hands, it can get in the way.

Also, as a consumer psychologist, you'd think I'd take the consumer more seriously. I've witnessed the creation of many superfluous and mind-numbing insights and research reports. It's okay to be bored; sometimes you need to sit through the boring bits to find new things or unlock new opportunities. The problem is these insights are often detrimental to brands.

The premise of this book is simple. Rather than listening to the consumer, try hearing your brand instead. Rather than consumer-led thinking, use brand-led thinking. Rather than being customer-obsessed, be brand obsessed. Rather than build human intelligence, build brand intelligence. What is brand intelligence? It's the ability of an individual or organisation to understand and prioritise the strength of the brand above everything else. The reason for this is straightforward — brand-led thinking builds a stronger, more valuable business. The formula my agency, Thinkerbell, uses is BXB4CX (or Brand Experience before Customer Experience). I explain this fully in chapter 7.

Finally, is it 'customer' or 'consumer'? Marketing is interested in both, and often they are one and the same. A customer is someone who buys the products or services, a consumer is the person who uses (or consumes) them. You can be both a customer and consumer, and the terms are often interchangeable. I use the description that feels most correct at the time of writing, which is normally 'consumer'. The other point to make is some people in marketing and business like to use the term 'human' or 'people' — which, of course, customers and consumers are. Marketers ultimately want people (or humans) to buy and use what we make, so I think it's a little disingenuous to call them 'people'.

Creating demand is vital for brands, whether it's encouraging consumers to buy more, or more consumers to buy or to pay more. Brands want demand-driven growth. To make sure your brand is relevant or motivating to consumers, who better to ask? The consumer, right? Wrong. Paradoxically this is where it starts to unravel. If you ask the consumer, listen to them and act on their advice, without prioritising the brand, then I'm sorry to say, but you're likely to be the architect of brand and business decline.

chapter 1
stop the consumer obsession

Businesses are currently obsessed with customers, consumer journey mapping and human-centred design. I believe your focus should be elsewhere: on understanding, defining and disseminating your brand throughout your organisation and to consumers. Prioritising the consumer over the brand erodes brand value and sets it on the path of homogenisation. Your brand will become just like the others. As you read this book, be open to the message to stop listening to the consumer and, instead, start to hear your brand.

Why do all cars look the same?

I recently bought a new car. During the protracted search, I became more and more confused as the brands, features, appearance and styles merged into one other. We wanted a family car with a bit of personality. This pretty low bar soon became a high bar. When I was a kid, I remember feeling proud as punch when my parents bought a Datsun 120Y. This was a car with power and grunt. And it was a radical shift from our previous car, a Fiat, which was seen as very exotic and European, particularly in Australia at the time. As a kid, I was into cars. Compared with today, the car back then had so much more character and functional differences.

But in the years that followed, something happened. Through globalisation and a flattening of consumer tastes, most cars are pretty much the same. Even car engines for different branded vehicles are made in the same factory. For example, the Volkswagen Golf GTI has the same engine as the Skoda Octavia RS. The Mercedes-Benz A180d has a dCi Renault diesel engine, which is also used by Nissan. It's the same story with the chassis, with similar frames rolling off the same lines for different brands.

Convergence isn't only happening with cars. Most products in the shops are similar. Cereal, tinned tomatoes and shampoo are similar. Branded and home-brand tortillas are often made by the same manufacturer with very little, if any, difference. Beer is similar. Insurance is similar. If you make an inquiry about your superannuation fund, the customer support services are often shared by several funds. At a functional level, brands are similar (if not exactly the same). Brands and businesses have become homogenised and it's a challenge for marketers to differentiate them.

The problem is more pronounced the more established the category, and the more established the brand is in that category. Take, for example, the Big Four banks in Australia. Most bank accounts are similar. The interest rate may vary slightly, but the offering is essentially the same whether you bank with Westpac, ANZ, Commonwealth or the NAB. Apart from the different-coloured logos (two of which use red), there's hardly any differentiation between them. But it wasn't always like this. Even banks once had distinctive and differentiated positions in the marketplace.

In addition to homogenisation, something else is happening. The fun bits of a car have disappeared. My wealthy uncle was a bit of a car fanatic, and I remember riding in a variety of them with him. Each was shaped differently, with unconventional design elements. Muscle cars of the 1970s had exaggerated bonnets. There were large tail fins on so-called 'Yank tanks'. The lime-green Porsche in the 1980s had a whale tail. You don't see these flourishes in car design any more. It's all so ... practical.

It's a similar story with architecture. In the foyers of banks from the Victorian era, wealth and opulence exuded from every corner, with elaborate cornices, ornate marble pillars and panelled wood walls. Or walk down a street of an inner-city suburb with houses from Victorian and even Georgian times: there are detailed flourishes and finishes everywhere. In the 1950s, it was common to have big curved walls within living spaces. Many of these design elements were not practical — they were artistic. Whereas buildings constructed today tend to all look the same as each other. The art and aesthetic has been removed. Buildings designed by architects who break away from the norm, such as Frank Gehry or Zaha Hadid, stand out because they are distinctive, with a vision that withstands practicalities, committees and possibly focus groups.

I see the same homogenisation process at play in politics: Australia's mainstream politicians lack vision. They are interchangeable middle-of-the-road people with interchangeable ideas. True, US President Donald Trump isn't from that mould, but I think he's an aberration. Politicians today are obsessed with polling and focus groups. In Australia, parties ditch leaders when they fail to win polls. Not election polls, but Newspoll, even though it got it very wrong in the 2019 federal election. Politicians seem to lead by consensus, not vision.

Let's apply this logic to my world of advertising and brands. These days, it can be a tough slog. In days gone by, advertising focused on entertainment and the creation of big responses. There were boundary-pushing themes (progressive and conservative) and campaigns were either so shocking, scary, charming or weird they were bound to get attention. This is mostly missing in the industry today.

It's not only advertising that's afflicted. The grit, beauty, romance or weirdness of pop culture has been shaved or chopped off in this sanitised, efficient and practical world. I believe the main reason this is happening is because of advertising's reliance on focus groups. Well, not focus groups alone; but I think there's an over-reliance on people's opinions at the expense of creating a vision and sticking with it.

Love him or loathe him, Steve Jobs had vision

Deft alignment is needed to make your business or organisation stand apart from the pack. In 1997, when Steve Jobs returned as CEO of Apple after 12 years away from the company, he told staff:

This is a very complicated world, it's a very noisy world. And we're not going to get the chance to get people to remember much about us. No company is. So, we have to be really clear about what we want them to know about us.

I'll repeat the important part: 'So, we have to be really clear about what we want them to know about us.' I love this. Jobs knew Apple had to fight against conformity and make the brand different from others in the personal computer market. Ensuring your brand is different and distinctive in the minds of consumers is difficult and takes enormous effort. The entire organisation needs to align behind this understanding and what the brand is aiming to achieve. Steve Jobs was amazing at instilling this within Apple.

'Every once in a while, a revolutionary product comes along that changes everything.' This is how Steve Jobs introduced the era-defining iPhone in 2007. And he wasn't wrong. In addition to its brilliant technology, Apple was smart in its naming protocol. It didn't come up with a complicated technical name for the new phone. As Mat Baxter, a friend and global CEO of media agency Initiative observed,

… the ability of Apple to use product names and language that was less technical and more human than its competitors' was a key differentiator, and proof point of its 'Think Different' brand positioning.

But something changed in 2017. The tenth-anniversary iteration of iPhone was named iPhone X. But consumers were confused. They called it the letter 'X' rather than Roman numeral ten. Mat is obsessed with technology companies and a keen observer of their fortunes. When

Apple broke its naming convention, he was mortified and wrote an article on LinkedIn saying,

> *Of course, product naming blunders can be forgiven. Perhaps someone in marketing felt the 'X' made the iPhone 10 feel appropriately special for its anniversary year. Or maybe it just looked better as an 'X' on the packaging and marketing materials. Whatever the reason, Apple had every opportunity to reset and get back on course with its famously simple and non-technical product names. Oh boy, did they stuff that up.*[2]

Mat suggests this small stuff-up is a signifier that Apple is becoming just like other technology companies. It has lost one of its points of differentiation — its naming convention. If Apple doesn't get its brand, what hope is there for the rest of us? For so long, Apple and Virgin, the world's consumer champions, have been held up as the benchmark of strong brands. But even great brands stray off course if not tightly and holistically managed. Apple's shift away from its previous naming convention was detrimental to the brand, and an indication the company is losing its way.

It's challenging to keep brands on course. The irony is the more you use the consumer as your rudder, and the more you ask them what they want, the easier it is to be thrown off course. You can end up creating something generic, vanilla and missing the interesting bits.

The customer is not the answer. Most of the time, the consumer doesn't even know what they want. As Henry Ford, founder of the Ford Motor Company, is reputed to have said, 'If I had asked people what they wanted, they would have said faster horses.' The more you listen to the consumer, the more your business or brand is in peril. And I predict that if you hear me out, you'll agree with me.

Customer obsession

Before I speak at conferences, I'm given a briefing. It's a real eye-opener as, over the course of an hour or so, I quickly learn about a business and then leave. The briefing is rarely conducted by someone in marketing;

usually it's someone organising the event or from internal culture or human resources. The briefings usually consist of me getting up to speed as quickly as possible on the business, the brand, its internal culture, key business challenges and opportunities, and the company's values. This rapid-fire induction within many companies puts me in the privileged position of gaining a deep insight.

One thing that often strikes me is how early the customer is mentioned. The challenge for many of the businesses I speak at is their desperation to 'get closer to the customer' and 'better understand the customer'. The phrases I hear over and over again are 'our business is customer-obsessed', or 'customer obsession is one of our values'. The other issue is people changing 'marketing' to 'consumer' or 'customer'. Marketers around the world are changing their work titles to Chief Customer Officer or Chief Audience Officer or Chief Consumer Officer. There are books promising tips and tricks on how to become customer-obsessed. No-one has changed their work title to be the Chief Brand Officer or created a central organising value that says 'be brand first'.

Marketing has always been about understanding your brand and your consumer and how they match up. But when I heard the term 'customer-obsessed' one too many times, I started thinking about why, and how widespread it is. This observation at speaking gigs wasn't the only reason for my concern. This is how global consultancy Accenture Interactive describes the role of the emerging Chief Marketing Officer (CMO):

> *They're making the customer central to their thinking and vision not just in the services they provide but also in how they adapt. They're building a customer-obsessed organisation, rewired from the inside-out with new technologies, new customer expectations and a new accelerated pace for change.*[3]

There's no mention of brand, marketing, demand or growth — only the customer. Further, they recommend 'Re-orientating and re-invigorating your organisation around the customer. Deliver hyper-relevant customer experiences at every touchpoint, building agility into the organisation to evolve to the changing needs of the customer.'[4]

This is a clear example, I believe, of getting things wrong. Customer obsession is not creating breakthrough thinking, nor is it creating stronger brands. It's inadvertently creating bland not brand-driven organisations. The recommendations of Accenture Interactive put way too much focus on listening to the consumer, and not on hearing your brand.

Some numbers behind customer obsession

After observing that brands are too customer-obsessed, I set out to discover why the old balance between understanding the brand and understanding the customer is now out of whack. In becoming customer-obsessed, many companies are losing the ability to remain brand-obsessed. To test the hypothesis, and better understand the issue, I asked marketers from around the world to complete a comprehensive survey about their behaviours with brand building and customer understanding. The survey was a self-reported questionnaire asking how they focus their time, effort and money when doing the job of marketing. From these behaviours, I could ascertain if customer obsession was taking hold and if brand obsession was suffering. Eighty-eight marketers completed the survey. Figure 1.1 got my attention.

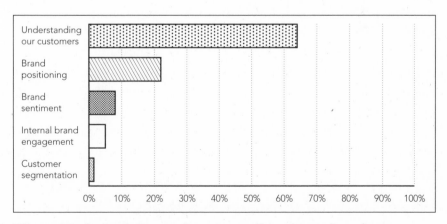

Figure 1.1: desired time and resource allocations of marketers

When asked if there was one thing they wanted to focus on and better understand, 62 per cent said 'understanding our customers', with only 22 per cent seeking to understand their brand. The dominance of consumer understanding at the expense of brand understanding was evident throughout the survey. In terms of dollars spent on understanding the brand versus the consumer, 22 per cent of respondents admitted to spending $0 last year in understanding the brand, while only 12 per cent spent $0 understanding the customer. Further, 72 per cent of respondents said it's 'extremely important to understand the customer' and only 48 per cent said it was 'extremely important to understand the brand'. When asked to explain why, here are some of the answers:

- 'They are the heart of success.'

- 'So you know you're going in the right direction.'

- 'They are the starting point for any brand success.'

- 'I work on the theory that the better we understand the customer, the better equipped we are to communicate with them in a way that engages them. That's the theory at least.'

- 'They are the reason we exist.'

- 'Because the customer pays our wages, not the brand.'

Consider these findings in a context where market research dominates conversations and briefings. When I started in this industry, marketing briefs were just that – brief. Today, they are accompanied by copious amounts of research and an inevitable warning: 'we have loads of research but little insight'. It's worrying to me that 62 per cent of marketers want to better understand the customer rather than their brand at a time when they understand their customers better than ever, or at least have the research to prove it. Customer obsession is driving strong brand thinking backwards.

Why is customer obsession happening?

When studying psychology, I was told the 'why' is not that useful. The issue of why I overeat doesn't stop me from overeating. What's needed is cognitive behavioural therapy, or changing thoughts and structuring my world in a way that makes it harder for me to eat. For example, I committed to following the principles of Intermittent Fasting and shared this with everyone I know, creating accountability. The question of 'why' customer obsession is happening is complex, and I only have half an answer. (But chapters 6 to 10 cover my solution to this obsession.)

One reason for a push towards the consumer over the brand is this: it's easier. Brands are complex and challenging. There's a belief by marketers that acting on what the consumer says is a safe bet. It's the modern equivalent of the adage 'Nobody gets fired for buying IBM'. In the 1960s and 1970s IBM was the market leader, so, when buying new software, you chose IBM over cheaper alternatives in the belief it was rock solid and would deliver. You couldn't go wrong. Today, marketers might believe they can't go wrong if consumer insights back their recommendations.

To understand why consumer obsession has taken off, I had a chat with a good friend, Mark Green, who has strong views on consumer obsession. Many years ago, Mark and I worked together at Saatchi & Saatchi. These days he heads up one of Australia's most successful agencies, Accenture Interactive The Monkeys, formerly known as 'The Monkeys'. Here's a summary of our chat (leading questions included):

Adam: Mark, why the obsession with the consumer today?

Mark: I think for those who lack conviction, relying on what the consumer says is a great middle-management tool. Because it's an opinion that they, the marketer, don't have. They are not starting from a position of understanding, certainty or confidence in their judgement, so, therefore, they'll resort to someone else's opinion as to what to do (the consumer).

Adam: So why don't you think they have certainty?

Mark: Well, brand management is about sacrifice. You have to stand for something, and that means not standing for a whole lot of other things. And inherent in that is a decision. And if you're not prepared to decide in the first place, you're sitting on the fence, and a lot of people like to sit on the fence.

Adam: OK.

Mark: You can't build the future from what's happened in the past. That's the leap where you need skill and conviction to try things that are different or haven't been done before. You have to have vision and confidence and skill.

Adam: Where does the skill come from?

Mark: Hmmm. It's the skill in understanding brands and what a brand stands for. And once you understand that, it's the skill in understanding how a brand connects with an audience. These are the skills that are lacking today.

Adam: Thanks, Mark.

Mark: Adam, do you want to try one of the new beers we've created?

Adam: Thanks, Mark.

I agree with Mark, particularly the point around 'skill'. It's rarer and rarer to find those who have the skills needed to define a brand.

How is customer obsession happening?

In the world of brand building, it's heresy to suggest you shouldn't listen to the consumer. I'm not saying market research is a waste of time (I'm neither brave enough nor stupid enough to suggest this). However, I think the balance between data collection and brand management is out of whack. Data is ubiquitous and omnipresent. The ability to measure everything a consumer does means knowledge about the consumer has increased, but knowledge of the brand has decreased. To complicate things, it's easiest to collect data from the most frequent users of your brand. Data is blinding marketers to strategic thinking and making them only look at the here and now. We're drowning in what many businesses are now building: a 'data lake'. (The name 'data lake' is probably a nerd joke about organisations striving to construct a data lake and then drowning in data.)

Figure 1.2 roughly shows the flow of marketing activity from strategy (thinking about tomorrow and how to get there) to execution and the things we need to measure and respond to today.

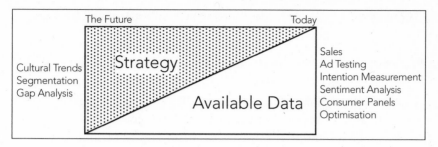

Figure 1.2: flow of marketing activity and available data

At all stages, it's possible to collect data and insights to inform decisions. However, transactional data (at the far right of the diagram) appears to be driving business decisions and helping us to live in a today-focused, short-term-thinking style of brand management. The 'Data' on the right-hand side refers to:

◆ Sales data, which can be broken into weekly, daily or hourly segments. It is this type of data that many in business are poring over. You might have been part of a Monday morning meeting eagerly assessing sales results from the previous week before optimising and tacking week to week.

◆ Ad testing, which is not reliable. Ad testing puts unfinished ads in front of consumers and asks them if the ad will make them buy. The ads are often presented in cartoon form and can get a little annoying. More on this later.

◆ Intention data, which is about whether the customer wants to buy your brand or product. Are they looking for it online? Have they visited the website or downloaded the app? Are they in the purchase funnel?

◆ Sentiment analysis, which is about how customers express their thoughts and feelings about your brand. But it's likely to be your customers saying these things, and therefore a very (in most cases) small percentage of your entire market.

◆ Consumer panels, which are online panels or Facebook groups companies consult with and ask questions. The customers are like pigeons in a Skinner Box, pecking at a response panel for their next gift card.

◆ Optimisation, which appears to make sense — but messaging (ads or communications) is often optimised for someone who has no intention of purchasing. Or, worse, has already purchased. How many times has an ad popped up on the internet after you've bought something?

Companies obsess about each of these insights. They attempt to work out how to turn an accidental click on a banner ad into an algorithm hell-bent on following you around the internet until you buy the product (or install an ad blocker). They obsess about short-term sales data rather than rallying the organisation around a brand idea. They get stuck in a weekly cycle of Monday morning numbers.

The data featured on the right-hand side of the figure doesn't help in understanding brands or in building long-term business strategies. This type of data can, however, determine the rhythm of business. It can suck time from what ultimately drives real value for the business, such as segmentation, gap analysis and brand positioning. These can be forgotten when marketers obsess about existing buyers or those about to buy their product. It is for these reasons that we are becoming even more customer-obsessed, as there is so much data available out there to collect.

It's tough to define what a brand stands for, and then to communicate the brand consistently in everything an organisation does. But this needs to be the priority of marketing. Examining the metrics of consumer data and sentiment risks creating generic and homogenised content. It is the enemy of distinctiveness.

Customer Obsession is Over

Customer insights, and understanding the customer wants and needs, are always going to be a part of what marketing is about. However, the abundance of consumer driven data, coupled with the increasing need to cover one's own ass, has made many a brand builder 'customer obsessed'. The next few chapters delve a little further into why that is such an issue.

chapter 2
consumers lie

French Enlightenment writer Voltaire encapsulates self-deception wonderfully with the line, 'Illusion is the first of all pleasures.[5]

Lying makes life better

Self-deception is a drug most of us mainline, numbing us to the harsh realities of life. For example, we are not as intelligent, smart, creative or honest as we think we are. This applies to ordinary abilities as well. Answer this question for me: Are you a below average, average or above-average driver? Forty years ago a study found that 93 per cent of Americans put themselves in the above-average category when it comes to driving ability, with only 7 per cent rating themselves as below average.[6] This finding has been repeated many times, and across many types of behaviours. It's called 'illusory superiority' and many of us suffer from it. In short, you think you're better than others, but it's an illusion; you're not.

Illusory superiority is also known as the above-average effect, the superiority bias, the leniency error, the sense of relative superiority and the primus inter pares effect. Self-deception is also manifest when considering harsh realities about the future. Put your hand up if you want to chat about how the world needs to respond when confronting climate change. As Al Gore declared, it's an inconvenient truth. How about the problem of wealth inequality? I'd guess that even reading about these challenges makes you feel uncomfortable.

Humans have an incredible ability for self-deception. We continually reinvent the past and turn imagination into fact. We are also terrible fortune-tellers and predictors of future behaviour. We just don't know. Asking people to predict and analyse their behaviour is very, very difficult. But it's what the $80 billion global market research industry is built upon. I worry that those working in the craft of marketing research, or who spend dollars commissioning research, are also lying to themselves about its value, and accuracy of the findings.

Bad men do what good men dream

My first job as a freshly minted psychologist was in the New South Wales prison system at the Oberon Correctional Centre. I needed to find somewhere to live and ended up flatting with another young prison psychologist, Steve Feelgood, who worked at nearby Kirkconnell Correctional Centre in nearby Bathurst. Steve was an interesting chap. Years before we met, he'd fallen asleep while studying, managed to knock over his bedside lamp, along with a glass of water, creating a live electrical current. For more than two hours, Steve's passed-out body slowly cooked as he lay in the small pool of water, burning the right side of his leg including his entire kneecap. Because of this, Steve wasn't very mobile. That, combined with the fact we didn't know many people, meant we spent a lot of time talking, writing about and living forensic psychology.

In addition to working at the prisons, we wrote a prison psychology newsletter called 'Borderline' and hosted a talkback radio show on 2MCE called 'Feelgood With Adam'. Get it? We were both intent on understanding what made people (mostly men) commit harmful and destructive behaviours. I made a deep dive into the dark side of the soul in my attempt to learn why 'bad men do what good men dream', to quote Robert Simon's popular forensic psychology textbook.

Steve believed we young psychologists working in the prison system were cannon fodder. Most of us chose to work there because NSW Corrective Services offered free supervision training, and supervision was mandatory for registration as a psychologist. After working there for just over two years, I left and joined a small private practice specialising in forensic psychology. I mostly interviewed and assessed sex offenders for the courts. The reports were usually requested by the defence team to build a case in favour of the alleged offender. (As an aside, the prosecution often couldn't afford to pay for psychological reports, so the only psychological report was written *for* the alleged offender. If you think this is an absurd situation I suggest you read Margaret Hagen's *Whores of the Court: The Fraud of Psychiatric Testimony and the Rape of American Justice.*)

The lawyers advised what I should and shouldn't include in my report; some were brazen while others gently tried to steer me to write what they wanted. If an alleged offender told me something that was too damning, I was encouraged to remove it because the lawyer wanted their client portrayed in the best possible light. When interviewing the men, I always asked about their offending behaviour and sexual paraphilias. (Generally speaking, the weirder their sexually related cognitions, the more of a danger they presented.)

So a young, relatively inexperienced psychologist is interviewing you for court. The interview has been arranged and paid for by your lawyer. The young psychologist asks, 'Have you ever had sex with animals?' Any guesses for what the 'correct' answer is? That's right: 'No.' Wouldn't saying 'yes' make you seem more dangerous or sexually odd? However, I was shocked at the number of men who would say, 'Yeah sometimes', or 'There was this one time' before describing a rather disturbing story indicating the man in question had some pretty concerning sexually related issues. They knew I was writing a report about them to be used in court, so why wouldn't they answer my question with a 'no'?

The reason is that no-one wants to see themselves in a negative light or for the world to think of them as a monster. These men certainly didn't want to see themselves as monsters or as harming anyone, especially children. As with all of us, they wanted to see themselves in the best possible light. This is human nature. So over the years, the men rationalised their sexual deviancies and harmful behaviours to themselves. Time and again, they told themselves their actions were acceptable. They rationalised their way through a cognitive maze of their making and didn't realise their answers were so distorted.

Talking with these men revealed to me that humans (all of us) are 'rationalising' creatures, not 'rational' creatures. We spend far more time rationalising our behaviour than we do in deciding to act rationally. By witnessing the operation of this process at an extreme level, it made it easier for me to observe this tendency in more mundane situations. The fact that we all want to paint the best possible picture of ourselves has never left me. It's one of the most useful and humbling things I learned working at the prison.

Why did you buy those shoes?

Let's assume you are reading or listening to this book wearing a pair of neat yet casual shoes. If I asked you to explain why you bought those shoes, I bet you wouldn't say, 'I'm wearing these shoes because I identify with the values of the brand', or 'When I wear this brand of shoes I fit in with an aspirational group of peers', or 'My boss wears this brand of shoe. If she notices I'm wearing them, she'll feel more positively about me'. So answer it now. Why did you buy those shoes?

I bet you answered, 'Because they are comfortable.' Women say this, even if wearing high heels. We rationalise our behaviour to portray ourselves in the best possible light and to avoid feeling like a goose. We purchase according to emotion but justify the purchase using reason.

Few want to admit to being susceptible to trends in marketing and advertising. But because humans are herd animals, we often go along with everyone else to fit in. You can read an excellent account of this inclination in Dan Gregory and Kieran Flanagan's 2014 book, *Selfish, Scared and Stupid*. We often lie to ourselves because, to be blunt, life is more comfortable that way. It amuses me when, in focus groups and dinner party conversations, people tell me they don't watch TV. And those who admit they do click on the remote are at pains to say they don't watch the ads. And in the final component of the triad of denial, they swear black and blue that the ads don't work on them. It's often common for some to go on a bit of a rant about how weird ads are, and then complain that ads should spell out what the product is and be done with it. Why would you have odd things like a gorilla playing the drums?

Most people assess a brand against how well the product or service meets the category need, because that's what they need, not your brand. Hence, a diverse array of insights will invariably get you to a place where your brand services the mean, or the amalgamation of everyone's opinions.

The three big issues with research

Market research asks people how they feel about products or services, and how they think they'll behave with regards to them. The information garnered through this process is often inaccurate because humans rationalise their behaviour, and because we don't act rationally. But there are several other more complicated forces at play. The most famous saying about market research in advertising circles is by David Ogilvy, the legendary founder of creative agency Ogilvy. He said, 'The problem with market research is that people don't think about how they feel, they don't say what they think, and they don't do what they say'. Let's break down David's critique step by step, because it provides an ideal framework for proving the inaccuracy of market research and the insights drawn from it.

1. People don't think about how they feel

Emotions drive most of our decision-making, with the brain processing emotions almost instantaneously. Dr Paul Ekman is the world's leading scholar in emotions and was a consultant on the Pixar film *Inside Out*. He describes six primary emotions: fear, anger, disgust, sadness, surprise and joy. Emotions are processed quickly as part of our survival mechanism. If you begin to swallow sour milk, you'll feel disgusted quickly enough to spit it out. If you see an attractive person, you'll feel it before you think 'that person is cute'. But we can't process and articulate these emotions as we feel them.

We generally feel the emotion and then fill in the cognitive gap. For example, if there's an 'instant attraction' between you and someone you've just met, you'll look for evidence to confirm that emotion. You'll say, 'Wow, we like the same movies, isn't that nice?', or 'Wow, we like different movies, isn't that nice?'. Applying this to the world of brands, we feel emotions when viewing advertising and beautiful products, but it's hard to articulate these emotions. This is especially the case in focus groups. If they can't describe how they feel, participants fill in the gaps with rational explanations. As Jonathan Haidt has said:

> *The conscious, rational brain is not the Oval Office; it isn't there making executive decisions in our minds. It is more like the Press Office, issuing explanations for decisions we have already taken.*

When filling out a survey or participating in a focus group, credence is given to the rational and explainable because that's what the consumer can articulate. Unfortunately, it's not how we make decisions.

2. People don't say what they think

Our self-concept encapsulates who we think we are — physically, emotionally, socially and spiritually. It drives how we present ourselves, how we act and what we say. Most of us think our self-concept (how we like to see ourselves) is how we are (actual self). If this was the case, then Actual Self (AS) = Ideal Self (IS). Unfortunately, there is often a gap between who we are and who we aspire to be. A focus group participant or someone completing a survey and questionnaire is more likely to answer according to their Ideal Self rather than their Actual Self.[7]

In psychological psychometric testing, questionnaires build in 'lie scales' to ascertain how much a subject is lying. However, there isn't time or money (or motivation) to develop sensitive tools for focus groups, or lie scales in quantitative measurement tools. Has a market research company researched the accuracy of market research? Have participants been asked if they have answered questions randomly to finish faster? How many people select only one brand because it means the questionnaire will be shorter? This information would make for more meaningful market research. In focus groups, it's common and normal for participants to say they don't watch TV, they read *The Guardian* newspaper and actively follow world politics. Most never admit an emotional rather than rational ad persuaded them to make a purchase. People present their Ideal Self, not the Actual Self. They don't say what they think, even to themselves, and especially not to a researcher.

3. People don't do what they say

Market research attempts to find out what people are planning to do and asks questions along the lines of, 'Is this more likely to make you buy X?' or 'Will you do X as requested by the communications?' Research conducted in this way is often inaccurate because consumers are bad at predicting their behaviour. If people did what they said they were going to do, intention to purchase would define every future consumer market. But it's quite a poor predictor of actual behaviour.

Focus groups are still a cornerstone of market research. They are usually conducted offline, with people invited to a venue with a one-way mirror for a two-hour conversation about a brand they may never think about again in their lives. They watch and respond to ideas and ads. Typical questions include, 'Who do you think this is targeting?', 'Do you think this would make you buy the brand?', 'Would you be more likely to consider this brand if you saw these ads?', 'Would you use this new product?' and 'Would you talk about this new product with your friends?' Up to a hundred or so questions are fired at these people as they project into the future and attempt to guess their anticipated behaviour.

There are many other social inconsistencies and biases to deal with, such as domineering respondents, or the type of respondent who'll drive an hour each way to attend a group on a cold, wet evening for $50, or the fact that the same people can end up attending hundreds of groups. In the industry, they are called groupies. The premise that focus group attendees can accurately anticipate the impact of messaging is the most significant inaccuracy of all.

A jaded senior qualitative market researcher once said to me, 'Adam, the only thing focus groups are useful for is for designing focus group rooms. Everything else is a waste of time.' When people are asked about the here and now they are more reliable. But who knows how you'll behave in the future? If you ask people if they like the room in which a focus group is taking place, they can answer honestly. But if you ask them if they're more likely to buy a particular type of insurance in the future if they view this specific ad, they wouldn't have a clue.

The gap between what people say in market research and what they actually do was identified as early as the 1970s. If intentions failed to match actions back then, the difference is even greater now because of increased choices, new technology and overall complexity. The 'purchase funnel' is far less a funnel and more a pinball machine, pinging us all over the place. It's not surprising that people's stated intentions fall by the wayside.

The paper 'When do purchase intentions predict sales?' in the *International Journal of Forecasting* found that many elements need to be in place for this to happen. The results indicate that intentions are more correlated with purchases[8]:

◆ for existing products, not new ones

◆ if the product is durable

◆ if the products are to be consumed/bought soon (not in the future)

◆ if the intention is for something particular, not vague.

There were other issues with the link between intention and sales, and these were primarily around measurement. What constitutes an intention? How do you link the intent to purchase? What are you comparing this data against?

TV viewing reveals the gap between what people say they do and what they do. Over the years, there have been predictions about the death of linear TV, with viewers claiming to watch far more streaming than broadcast TV. Poor research design saw a series of outlandish claims from the digital disruptors that simply never materialised. This happened partly because skewed samples of context-sensitive questions combined with misguided analysis to generate misleading conclusions. But it's also because respondents are much more likely to remember new experiences (streaming), and are unable to remember the number of hours they spent watching traditional broadcast TV. They said they watched more hours of on-demand and online TV than broadcast TV, but it is a far cry from their actual behaviour.

Here are Rory's thoughts on consumer insights and market research:

My general advice here is that you should spend a great deal of time, money and effort hearing consumers. But you shouldn't spend too much time listening to them. A very good principle in problem-solving is that you should not spend a minute trying to solve a problem until you have spent a day trying to redefine it. And so hearing the consumer is a very good idea. It's a good idea because consumers are alert to problems to which businesses may be entirely deaf. That's important. The fact that people are upset about something really matters. But listening to customers can be highly misleading. They don't always know what they are upset about. And they certainly can't always explain what the solution may be. In post-rationalising their emotional state, consumers have already framed the problem in a rational context. But this may bear very little relation to the real reason that gave rise to their feelings, and so may be almost useless in helping you define the real problem to be solved.

To demonstrate the difference between listening and hearing, Rory references a scene from the terrible 1990s movie *White Men Can't Jump*. Wesley Snipes' character, Sidney Deane, and Woody Harrelson's character, Billy Hoyle, start arguing in the car when 'Purple Haze' by Jimi Hendrix plays on the cassette player (yes, times have changed). Deane says white people can listen to Hendrix but can't hear it because Hendrix was a black artist making music for black people. He says, 'Look, man, you can listen to Jimi, but you can't hear him. There's a difference. Just because you're listening to him doesn't mean you're hearing him.' The takeaway: don't listen to what people say, but hear what's behind what they say. Hear the real problem for which they want a solution. In the next two chapters, I'll explain that even if you hear the consumer, delivering on what they want may remove value from your brand and banish it to homogeneity. But more on that later. Rory's insights (and referencing of the movie *White Men Can't Jump*) helped me to develop the title of this book.

Would you rather a brand donates money to charity or spends money on advertising?

Imagine you are a participant in a focus group or completing an online questionnaire, and you view two ads for a familiar brand of household cleaner. In the first ad, the brand features the same jingle as always, shows the product at work and introduces a funny new tagline. In the second ad, the brand promises to give $250 000 to a charity if you buy this brand during a specific time frame. Which ad do you prefer?

I faced this scenario not long ago. The client wanted to test which ad people favoured — the one that matched what the brand had done for years or the alternative. The focus group chose the alternative — give money to charity. But this arguably wasn't the best strategy for the brand's advertising. Consumers might like that the brand donated $250 000 to charity. But would it make them buy the brand? And could the alternative, the 'brand ad', be more persuasive?

Research is very episodic and measures the here and now. Consumers in the research group were not shown the brand's history or given the ability to articulate which ad would be better for the long-term strength of the brand. Our conversations with the research agency were heated as they talked about benchmarks and their ability to predict consumer reactions. After numerous conversations, we chose to ignore the research and created the 'brand ad'. Fortunately, it's performed exceptionally well, sales increased and the brand's distinctive assets are impressed into the minds of consumers.

In research, consumers make assessments based on how they think others will perceive them and how they want to see themselves. They're not trained or skilled in speaking on behalf of what's best for the brand. The less you ask and the more you observe, the better.

Does behaviour lie?

Behaviour doesn't lie, but it can be deceptive. It's become fashionable in the world of marketing and marketing research to attempt to avoid the lie by focusing on behaviours. This is because of the significant amount of data now available and the ability to easily test everything. Those relying on 'behaviours' for insights might be smugly thinking this chapter doesn't relate to them because they don't ask the consumer about anything. Unfortunately for the hardcore behaviourists who like to test everything, I think their situation is a little worse. Behaviours don't lie, but they can deceive.

One common form of deception is brands and businesses that put substantial effort into 'engagement' in social channels. Engagement measures how often people like, share, react and comment on a brand. There are a few issues with this. Many engagement measures don't take into account positive and negative sentiment. The main issue is it has zero correlation with business growth. Even Facebook's official documents warn against valuing engagement saying, '...in many cases, these click-based forms of engagement do not align with the desired business outcomes of your content.'[9]

What about something more reliable than engagement behaviour? What about sales behaviour? This can also be deceptive. Peter Field, the world's marketing effectiveness silverback, examined the relationship between brand-building creativity and sales for the Institute of Practitioners in Advertising. Titled 'The Crisis in Creative Effectiveness', it reveals how marketing is increasingly characterised by campaign short-termism, with creative juries rewarding work that generates short-term sales but ignores the long-term health of the brand. As the report concludes, the industry has '...arrived in an era where award-winning creativity typically brings little or no effectiveness advantage.'

They're not the only ones who lie

It's not just consumers who can't be trusted. It's not only in the frivolous world of advertising that people behave in ways that appear entirely irrational. As I mentioned at the beginning of this chapter, I witnessed it with prisoners in the legal system. However, it also applies to those who wield the gavel. My father was a judge, as was my father-in-law. I know that judges, even more than advertising types, believe their hype. But in their case, the hype is that they're rational, logical, humble and conservative. They don't take risks, and they only act on the evidence. Judges are the very embodiment of reason and reasoning in our society. However, I've been around enough of them to know this isn't always the case.

A fascinating study in 2011 found judges handed out harsher sentences before lunch.[6] The reason is that they're hungry and, after a busy morning, their mental resources are depleted. After they have a bite to eat and feel replenished, the judgements return to the norm. They are human, after all. The study shows that influences outside of our control cause our behaviour: 'Our findings suggest that judicial rulings can be swayed by extraneous variables that should have no bearing on legal decisions.'

If you asked a judge if they were more lenient because they were in a good mood with a full tummy, they would reject the notion out of hand. Judges sees themselves as rational human beings above such trivialities. It's a lovely example of how inaccurate our 'judgements' can be and how open to suggestion and influence we are. If we can't trust a judge to make an accurate decision, how on earth can we trust the consumer to predict the future?

Beating the lie

So market research is inaccurate. Everyone knows it is. It isn't like 'science', which is objective. There is generally vested interest in the answers, and often the research company is trying to protect their commercial interests and seem relevant despite woefully out-of-date methodologies. Or it could be the commissioning business just wants to find supporting evidence to go ahead with an idea; this is more akin to gathering confirmatory evidence than research.

The lies people tell themselves get in the way of brand-building marketing. Therefore, it's a question of how to properly conduct research. I'm imploring you to put brand thinking ahead of consumer thinking, but I don't want you to stop using research completely. I asked one of the best marketing researchers I know, Wiemer Snijders, what he suggests for those who need to do research and better understand the customer.

Wiemer told me a story about buying a new car. The salesperson told him some of the car's features were created after consulting with car users. People suggested storage for a laptop and a hook for groceries so they wouldn't topple over. Wiemer was baffled that the salesperson seemed to think he had just offered him a critical insider tip, and said,

> *Be careful when it comes to listening to consumers. Not everything people say they want is what they value enough to buy when it comes to it. We are selling; we have to filter what the end-user says and the data we collect with commercial sense.*

Wiemer says three things have helped him determine whether to pay attention to consumer research — or ignore it. The first is timely answers.

> *People are terrible at predicting what they'll do in the future, so we need to be wary of this type of information. If we do ask people about their future buying behaviour, we should refer to an appropriate time frame — which will vary by category.*

If asking people how likely it is they'll switch to a different insurance provider, ask in the month before renewal rather than six months ahead. People will happily offer an inaccurate opinion if they have no skin in the game. It's just pretend and hypothetical to them. What does it matter if they lead you down the garden path? If possible, make it real for them. If you're researching the type of drink they want, then also conduct research when they're actually thirsty and about to buy a drink.

Secondly, randomness in samples can be a trap. A/B testing may be a useful way of screening potential improvements; it measures what people prefer. However, many tests don't last long enough to match the full purchase cycle or offer enough data points:

It means running the risk of misinterpreting short-term results because you've potentially failed to measure the regression to the norm. It's a bit like walking up a hill and stopping before reaching the top. You fail to see what more there is and can miss the real conclusion.

Thirdly, size matters. Many so-called insights from research ask people what they think or feel, without relating it to actual buying behaviour:

This means that if we don't control for brand size or user type in brand image tracking data, we will likely miss the primary learning. Brands may, for example, seem more differentiated than they indeed are, leading managers to do things that focus too narrowly and may hurt sales and profitability.

What people say and do can be two very different things. And did Wiemer buy the car with the add-ons? No, he bought the standard one. My take-home message: where possible, watch people rather than ask them about predicted behaviour.

These are the typical methods in market research:

- *In-depth interviews.* A person is interviewed one-on-one about a particular issue or brand.

- *Focus groups.* A small group of people discuss an issue or brand. The conversation follows a free discussion guide, moderated by a researcher.

- *Surveys.* Questions and prompts that ask a predetermined set of people how they think and feel about a particular brand or issue.

- *Questionnaires.* People respond to a series of questions, either online or over the phone about a brand or issue.

But as this chapter has illustrated, each method has pros and cons associated with it. Even when they receive money, people lie and don't answer questions honestly. The research is laden with inaccuracies, costs and quality issues, and, in many cases, the costs far exceed the benefits. Research is now shifting into:

◆ behavioural research

◆ participatory research

◆ artificial intelligence.

Behavioural research looks at how people interact with the product or service in their environment. Technology allows the researcher to better understand how the product, service or brand could be adapted to meet the needs of the consumer. It involves spending time with consumers and watching them interact and use the product in situ. Companies such as Watch Me Think ask people to film themselves using the product and discuss its pros and cons. They're not interviewed, they simply do a talking review. Lookback.com does a similar thing with online and digital brands. You can watch people using your product in real life situations.

With participatory research marketers are attempting to close the gap between the producer and the consumer through what's known as 'end-user innovation'. Give consumers examples of your product, and they'll innovate, customise or improve it in some way until it matches their needs.

'Artificial intelligence' will seem far less magical and far more practical if you replace the term 'artificial intelligence' with 'computer program'. Artificial intelligence helps to process the swarms and lakes of data to develop insights into how people behave, think and feel about various brands and issues.

It's essential that strong marketing has insight embedded throughout it. But the insight needs to serve the brand and not the other way around. If your insights rely on revealed truths rather than people anticipating their future behaviour, it'll reduce your risk of insights corrupting the entire marketing process.

It's a wrap

A good starting point with consumer insight is this: don't believe the consumer. Their deception and lies can be avoided but not eliminated. Another point to emphasise is don't let the tail wag the dog. Research and insights should be subservient to the brand and what it needs to do, not what consumers like and especially not what they predict they'll like.

To avoid being deceived do these three things:

1. Construct your research to feel real to people, so they'll care.

2. Be timely.

3. Watch, don't ask.

chapter 3
listening to the consumer eliminates value

'I love brands. I love it when they advertise to me and encourage me to visit their website. In fact, the more I see of their advertising and the more time I spend on their website, the better!'

Who has ever said this? I believe the answer is, 'No-one, ever.' Unless your brand caters to fanatics, such as sports enthusiasts or fashionistas, most people don't want to be bothered by most brands, most of the time. I estimate that consumers think about your particular brand somewhere between 0.00 per cent and 0.01 per cent of the time. People don't care about brands, especially your brand.

Think about what 'consumer-centric' means. If you put what the consumer wants and needs at the heart of your business, would your brand even exist? If it existed, would it advertise? If it advertised, would it advertise often? Understanding what the consumer wants and needs and genuinely delivering on it might mean your brand doesn't exist at all. Sorry, but someone has to say it.

Dinner with Gladwell

Malcolm Gladwell is a best-selling author and way ahead of his time in describing today's holy grail: going viral. His first book, *The Tipping Point*, argues that trends operate in the same way as an epidemic. The book starts with the fascinating story of old-fashioned shoe brand Hush Puppies unexpectedly becoming the shoe of choice for downtown Manhattan hipsters. This trend was picked up by key fashion designers and eventually led to the shoes being available in every shopping mall in America. As Gladwell writes,

> *Ideas, products, messages and behaviours spread just like viruses do. Their chief characteristics — one, contagiousness; two, the fact that little causes can have big effects; and three, that change happens not gradually but at one dramatic moment — are the same three principles that define how measles moves through a school or flu attacks every winter.*

When I discovered he was coming to Australia for a speaking event, I emailed his assistant with an invitation for dinner at Tetsuya's, a top-end Japanese restaurant in Sydney. To my shock, he accepted. Around the table, among others, were Dennis Paphitis, founder of Aesop; Paul Bassat, CEO of Seek; Charmaine England, the then marketing director of Unilever; and Karen Wong, marketing director of Coca-Cola. This interesting bunch of people are keenly interested in understanding the consumer.

After some small talk, the table asked Gladwell questions ranging from 'Should brands have a purpose?' to 'How should brands spend their advertising dollar?' He answered the questions with humility and insight in a slightly tired, jaded and flat voice. Finally, someone asked this question: 'What do you think people want from brands?' The simple question elicited an even more straightforward answer. After a quiet pause Gladwell said: 'People want to be left alone.' According to Gladwell, people don't want brands to entertain them, to have a higher purpose, to create content or to advertise. Brands, he argued, should be available when the consumer wants or needs them.

It was a refreshingly honest perspective. People in business like to think their product or service is held dear in the consumer's heart. There are exceptions, but for most consumers, this isn't the case. Most go about their day, not caring about your brand or the category that your brand operates in. They want to be left alone. Makes sense, right? I call this the 'Consumer in Control' model, which is detrimental to business. Here's why.

Consumer in Control

In this model, we are only in consumers' lives on their terms. When the consumer is in control, both 1) advertising and communications, and 2) developing the actual product or service are under threat, a situation that ultimately removes value from your brand. Let me explain.

Advertising with the Consumer in Control

Imagine if we could advertise to a consumer when they wanted us to. In this scenario, they can view a hyper-targeted, hyper-personalised ad in the moments before purchase. Once viewed, the ad disappears, never to be seen again by them or anyone else. Does this sound like personalised advertising nirvana and a much cleaner communications landscape? To me, it seems like some kind of hell. Further, a hell that will destroy brands and businesses.

There's a glimpse of this horror in the wild film *Minority Report* released in 2002. Tom Cruise's character walks into a Gap store, and a virtual digital assistant asks if he likes the 'assorted tank tops' he bought last week. Personalised digital ads also bombard Cruise as he walks through a screen-lined lobby. This imaginary world was seen as scary and dystopian when the film was released. Today, it doesn't seem so far-fetched. My friend Faris Yakob also happens to be a futurist. He wonders why, if most people see *Minority Report* as a dystopian view of the future where free will evaporates, our advertising friends think it's nirvana?

The broader business and marketing community is becoming very excited about the idea of 'personalisation' of messaging, and messaging only where and when the consumer wants it. However, I'm not aware of any research that says people want to be advertised to in this way, or that hyper-personalised advertising is a good way to build a brand or business. Just because we have the ability to do more personalised and targeted communications doesn't mean we have to use it.

In 2005, *The Journal of Advertising Research* published an interesting article by Tim Ambler titled, 'The Waste in Advertising Is the Part that Works'.[11] Ambler argues that consumers believe a brand is of a higher quality if they think a lot of money was spent on it. The waste in advertising — from expensive production costs to extravagant media spends blasting the same message to everyone — works in the same way as the handicap principle in nature.

The handicap principle is a beautiful concept best described using peacocks as an example. When a male peacock displays its luxurious plumage, he signals that he has plenty of resources at his disposal and therefore he is fitter, sexier and better than his competition. The same principle is at work when a person spends a large amount of money on a sports car. It signals that because they can afford an expensive, silly car, they must have an abundance of resources — money — at their disposal.

Ambler argues this principle operates in advertising. Big productions and high media spend signal to the consumer that the brand is serious and confident of future success. This can't be achieved in hyper-targeted advertisements. In a world of the Consumer in Control, we don't know how the consumer hears about our brand. No consumer in control will choose to be consistently advertised to, and yet, as I'll get into, this is the premise for how brands grow.

Byron Sharp wouldn't be happy

Listening to the consumer, only appearing when they want you to and making things as easy as possible is not only wrong, it's the opposite of how marketing works. As the modern master of marketing, Professor Byron Sharp, puts it, 'No marketing activity, including innovation, should be seen as a goal in itself, its goal is to hold on to or improve mental and physical availability.'[12] According to Sharp, mental and physical availability is the key to brand growth.

Following this thinking, a marketer's job is twofold. Firstly, to ensure a brand becomes stuck in consumers' minds and is easy to recall when they need the category that the brand falls within (e.g. when someone thinks, 'Gosh I'm thirsty', a marketer's job is to ensure that the person thinks of their brand before any other). This is called 'mental availability'. Secondly, if the brand is easy to remember (that is, there's mental availability), then they must ensure that there is physical availability too: the brand must be easily bought or consumed. So if we build on the previous example, the person thinks, 'Gosh I'm thirsty', then the marketer ensures there's mental availability (that is, their brand is thought of first) and that there is physical availability (that is, it's easy for the consumer to get that particular brand). All of this can be summed up in Coca-Cola's global strategy from some years ago, which they described as being 'within arms-reach of desire'. The 'arms reach' speaks to physical availability; the 'desire' speaks to mental availability.

With regards to mental availability, Sharp told me over dinner,

Adam, there are two fundamental rules about how to spend your advertising budget. Rule number one is spend as much as you can. And rule number two is to divide your total spend and spend around a twelfth of it every month.

Here Byron is making the point that in order to stay 'top of mind' you need to constantly remind consumers of your presence, and you never quite know when the need will ignite. If you ask the consumer what they want, they won't say 'constantly advertise to me'. We all know they say something closer to the opposite.

There is another issue with the hyper-targeted Consumer in Control approach to advertising: your brand will not grow. You see, you'll only reach your existing customers because potential customers don't know you exist, so they'll never want you to advertise. In most consumer product categories, the user spread follows a negative binomial distribution (NBD). This is a statistically predictable distribution curve first discovered by Professor Andrew Ehrenberg. This model suggests that across all categories, a few people buy a significant portion of your brand, but most buy the brand infrequently. The figure 3.1 (overleaf) was created by my friend Wiemer Snijders, whom I introduced in chapter 2. It's from the non-alcoholic beverages category, indicating the typical customer base for a popular brand. The graph shows the number of people that buy a particular brand within the category throughout the year.

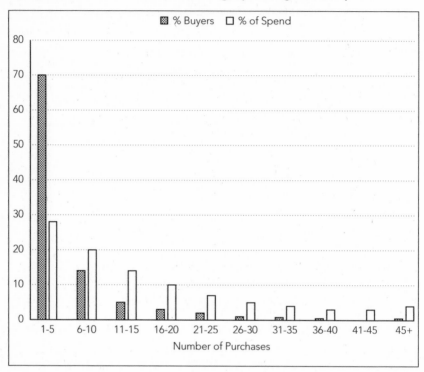

Figure 3.1: a lot buy a little, a little buy a lot

Source: The Commercial Works client data, beverages, 2016, 52 weeks' buying

As Snijders tells us,

> *The brand is well known, yet almost three-quarters of its buyers bought it five times or less, together realising nearly 30% of annual sales. This seems surprising, yet marketing science says that it is quite normal. The pattern is closely predicted by a statistical curve, the negative binomial distribution or NBD. Every brand's customer base is like this... This pattern in buying behaviour is so regular that it can be successfully modelled, and the predicted values used to understand and benchmark actual or future brand performance measures.[13]*

Snijders argues the negative binomial distribution is the statistical pattern that underpins much of the evidence presented in Byron Sharp's game-changing 2010 book *How Brands Grow*. I recommend the book highly.

It's likely your brand acts in this way as well. Wiemer points out, 'In 60 years of research, no brands — from global market leaders to startup challengers —have been found with anything other than NBD loyalty.'

Without the knowledge that most people buy a brand infrequently, businesses run the risk of listening to the wrong consumer. In fact, they often only listen to those with the loudest voices who are invariably the biggest users in the category. These are the ones who are vocal on social media channels. Many businesses put together their own consumer panels featuring medium to heavy users of the brand. However, it's likely the business already meets the needs of these consumers. Instead, the brand should focus on appealing to light users and those who have never bought the good or service. This is also where their advertising budget should go — to keep on penetrating into new and emerging buyers of the category. Getting data on these people before they've entered the category is really hard — hence again there is a need for broadcast communication that's always on and appears to have lots of 'wastage'.

GME is an Australian company that designs and manufactures emergency beacons and radio communication devices, such as CB radios, with a reputation for being rugged and tough. Their core customers are off-road 4WD enthusiasts. If the company creates a product that's considered 'soft' or contrary to the needs of hard-core adventurers, their loyal but small customer base complains. As a consequence, GME's customer base has remained very niche because it resisted innovating or targeting new consumers. Unfortunately for them, other companies have entered the CB radio market with a more contemporary offering and have won significant market share. For example, CB radio manufacturer Uniden has cute two-way radios for adults and kids to play with together. They are just a bit of fun and more like a toy than a serious CB radio. However, when these kids grow up, they'll be more likely to think of Uniden rather than GME if they're in the market for a CB radio. GME is still a strong brand with a very loyal following in part because of the superior quality of its products. However, it will be interesting to see how they evolve and chase a new group of consumers. In many cases, companies should pay less attention to their core consumer because it prevents them from focusing on new customers.

Personal communication isn't all it's cracked up to be

In our quest to personalise brands and give consumers attention, marketers spend time, effort and money building a 'personalised relationship' with the people they 'meet'. By 'meeting', I mean have you ever clicked on a pop-up ad or visited a website only to be stalked on the internet by annoying ads? Those ads are delivered programmatically. The advertising algorithm knows a bit about you and why you visited, and the creative messaging is tailored to you and will continue to pop up wherever you are on the internet. You might go online looking for shoes. Days, weeks and months later, you are bombarded with ads for shoes. The impact of personalised communications is still pretty ropey. I doubt many consumers would request personalised ads. In fact, most people think they are kind of creepy.

Personalising consumer messaging has several issues:

◆ The consumer doesn't care about your brand, and advertising is a poor tool to convince people of anything. Advertising is a long-term game. It works by creating little impressions of the brand, and those impressions come along with associations. We are not as susceptible to advertising as some snake oil salesmen would like us to think. The last thing most people want to deal with is a targeted ad or conversation.

◆ Advertising is most effective when it 'seeps' into the minds of consumers. It's the reason why occasionally it makes you laugh. When we make people laugh and feel good, their defences come down and we can create a positive impression. The personalised information is more aggressive. Robert Heath examines how successful advertising drips into the consumer's mind and doesn't become caught in an argument.[14]

◆ Aggressive selling causes 'reactance'. How do you react when someone strongly argues a point with you? You probably respond defensively and mount a counter-argument, even if it's just in your head. You are building what psychologists call 'reactance to messaging'. Reactance happens when someone feels they have limited choices or alternatives. Look at figure 3.2. This is what happens when advertising tries too hard.

Figure 3.2: when advertising tries too hard

Source: Photo by Katherine Hood on Unsplash

Monkey see, monkey do: advertising also works by creating a social norm and showing consumers what's trending in popular culture. This creates an 'assumptive social norm'. People believe something is popular because it's widely advertised, which suggests everyone else must be buying it. This informed the messaging for Foxtel with its tagline, 'We're a Foxsporting Nation': it gave the impression that everyone was subscribing to Foxtel. Social norming is impossible to achieve through personalisation because of its application — changes in societal attitudes can't happen through messaging crafted to the individual.

Personalisation focuses on the wrong people. Personalisation only occurs within an audience that is already purchasing (or thinking about purchasing) that brand, which leaves the rest of the market untouched. It's the opportunity cost of personalising your brand with people who have a relationship with you anyway, versus the mass market, which is where the opportunity lies for most businesses. This was the case with GME.

Product and service design with the Consumer in Control

Imagine a scenario in which you listen to the consumer and create a website, app or digital experience that's intuitive and easy to use; they can enter, exit and find what they need in one click or swipe or voice-activated control. If you work in web design, I'm sure you've come across Steve Krug's book *Don't Make Me Think*. Web designers aim to make navigating a website as easy as possible by considering where people look on the screen for information, how many clicks it takes to make a purchase and how to create clear 'calls to action'. This logic is now being applied to brands. The belief is, the easier it is to enter and exit your brand experience, the more consumers will like you and reward you with continued patronage.

Daniel Kahneman is a psychologist and Nobel Prize winner. His 2011 best-selling book *Thinking, Fast and Slow* outlines the two systems that drive the way we think. Kahneman describes these as System 1 and System 2. System 1 is fast, intuitive and emotional. It's like a super computer operating on intuition, experience and gut feel, processing 11 billion bits of information a second and instantly jumping to a solution. System 2 is slow, lazy and sequential. It's super smart but requires significant effort to work through problems. It only processes about 40 billion bits of information per second and is exhausting to run.

The book is a brutal, slow read because it's very dense and filled with information better suited to System 2 thinking. I reviewed the book for *The International Journal of Advertising*, but in truth I didn't finish reading it because it was too long and a little too boring for me. I wish Kahneman had written the book for System 1 thinkers, with more stories, more emotion and more repetition of key information.

Even though the brain makes up about 2 per cent of total body weight, it accounts for around 20 per cent of energy usage. Humans are built to conserve energy and not to burn energy unnecessarily. When it comes to thinking, we take the path of least resistance. This is System 1 in action: fast, intuitive and going with the flow. If we are presented with two chocolate bars and one is easier to reach, we'll choose the one that's easier to reach. If one of the chocolate bars is perceived to be more popular, we'll select that one in the belief that it's better. If we've eaten one of the chocolate bars before, we're more likely to choose it again. If we've seen an advertisement for a chocolate bar, we're more likely to choose it because it's familiar. The brain is continually searching for shortcuts to conserve energy, and these shortcuts can lead to what's known as cognitive biases. This leads marketers to embrace content that has a high degree of cognitive fluency.

Cognitive fluency is the ease with which we process information and determine what that information means. It refers not only to the experience of a task or processing information, but the feeling people associate with that task. We are more likely to remember and believe information if it's easy to process.

However, there's an equal and opposite concept known as cognitive disfluency, which is the enemy of human-centred designers and Steve Krug devotees. It says we process information depending on the required effort and if it's easy (fluent), we find it much more pleasant than if it's difficult (disfluent).

Why human-centred design is killing brands

It's not only advertising and web design that's putting the consumer at the centre. Human-centred design (HCD) is a design and management framework that considers the human perspective during the problem-solving process. The brand, product or service is designed from the user's perspective. It observes the problem within the user's context then brainstorms, conceptualises, develops and implements a solution. HCD emerged from Design Science and Ergonomics.

As an aside, I studied Ergonomics at Murdoch University, for which I received my only undergraduate A grade. I observed that when you turn the tap on in the shower, you need to reach under the showerhead and as a consequence, you get blasted with cold water. Despite my undergraduate breakthrough, the shower at my house still has the tap located behind the showerhead. Every morning, I think of ergonomics, my A grade and the fact that because it's cheaper and easier to run the tap from the same water pipe as the showerhead, we are destined to have poorly designed showers. I'm pleased to hear many showers built today have mixer taps to the side. One day I hope to enjoy this design at my home.

If you want to read more about HCD, head to ideo.com. IDEO is a global design company that wants to answer some of the world's big questions (such as how to navigate disruption and thrive in changing times) using design.

Watching IDEO's Paul Bennett in a TED talk informed my understanding of HCD. Bennett talks about being asked by a healthcare system in Minnesota to describe what the patient experiences. He said the healthcare team had expected to be shown a series of graphs and Powerpoint presentations, but instead, IDEO showed them a video of a hospital ceiling. This, the team said, is the patient experience at most hospitals — staring at a grey polystyrene ceiling with yellow lights. Following this insight, the healthcare team made several small but significant changes, including decorating the ceiling. Watching the video reminded me of hospital visits during my childhood because of bad asthma. The ceiling consisted of fitted ceiling squares with loads of little holes in them. I spent many days counting the number of holes in the ceiling with the aim of not losing count. Because there were thousands of holes, I invariably lost count, but it kept me entertained as I lay there, short of breath, for hours on end. I empathised strongly with the IDEO case study.

Because HCD has many interesting applications, it might be challenging to recognise how HCD is killing brands and businesses. Let me explain.

This is a typical process using Human-centred design (HCD).

1. *Empathise.* Understand the consumer and the context within which they use the product or service.

2. *Define.* Articulate a problem to be solved. Theme insights from stage 1, cluster the findings, weigh up which areas of use or interaction between product and consumer you want to address.

3. *Ideate.* This is about developing ideas that overcome the barrier or harness the opportunity identified in stage 2. A long list of ideas is generated and refined through a grading and prioritisation exercise.

4. *Prototype.* Develop an MVP (minimal viable product) from the one or two ideas that float to the top.

5. *Test.* These prototypes are tested and evaluated.

This process puts the consumer at the centre and takes an empathic approach to design. But there's a significant flaw. Where does a 'brand' fit in this process? I'm sure if you work in the industry you'll be able to define where brand thinking comes in, but it's rarely if ever documented. Of all the HCD processes on the market, I couldn't find one that had the brand as its core or North Star. That's not to say it can't be added. I'm sure it can. However, brand thinking, both philosophically and practically, is not part of HCD and, on the rare occasions it is, it's certainly not the core of it. I think that many in the HCD community still shudder at the thought of the brand like it's a dirty word. It's not 'cool'.

To be blunt, HCD is not about building brands or businesses. It's about creating a more efficient and seamless world for the consumer. You could argue it's about eliminating friction and creating a more streamlined and efficient user experience. There's that word again, 'efficiency'. Consumers don't really need flourishes like wide fins on their cars, they don't need moments of play on a website that stop them from entering certain areas until they complete a fun task, and people certainly didn't need the myriad fonts that were available on Apple computers when they launched.

The whole premise of having to find a problem to fix before applying creativity worries me too. It leads to efficiency, but not breakthrough thinking. HCD is like a truck slowly moving along a pot-holled street fixing the holes as they see them one by one — it's a terribly inefficient way to rebuild a road, let alone a business.

Let's imagine a future in which all brands, products and services have HCD principles applied to them. Brands are as 'efficient' as possible, as they understand the consumer more and build a product or service around what they want — not what's best for the brand. Here's what could happen — I call it creating a Teflon brand.

How to create a Teflon brand

Imagine you're the CEO of Twitter and it's 2017. You're worried about the drop-off rates of tweets and you want to make the experience a little easier for consumers. You want less friction and you want to not make people think too hard. You conduct a HCD study to inform the product development of your platform. Here's my fly-on-the-wall imagining of this process:

1. *Empathise.* Twitter's data indicates usage drops off when people find they can't express themselves in 140 characters. It happens when people are in a time-pressured situation — such as using Twitter while watching TV. Twitter decides the pain point is the restriction to 140 characters.

2. *Define.* Allow Twitter users to use more than 140 characters.

3. *Ideate.* Suggestions include removing the word limit entirely or slightly increasing the character limit.

4. *Prototype.* Options are prototyped and tested with consumers.

5. *Test.* A decision is made to double the number of Twitter characters to 280.

And that's exactly what Twitter did in a bid to stop people getting annoyed because they couldn't say everything they wanted to in a short tweet. Before they made the change, research companies measured the proposed impact and found most people felt positive about the increase.[15]

Now, imagine that during these discussions someone said, 'Oh you can't do that. Twitter's brand is tightly aligned to 140 characters', with another person chiming in with, 'The 140-character limit comes from the days of SMS limits of 160 characters. People don't remember this, but the logic is pretty cool.' Reflections such as these don't come up in a usability lab or a focus group.

Twitter research showed that increasing the character count from 140 to 280 didn't change the length of most Twitter posts. For those who like stats: 'Only 5% of Tweets sent were longer than 140 characters and only 2% were over 190 characters.'[16] But one thing certainly changed. Twitter compromised its unique selling proposition (USP), or central organising thought. A platform celebrating brevity suddenly doubled the length of tweets. Author JK Rowling wrote of the decision: 'Twitter's destroyed its USP. The whole point for me was how inventive people could be within that concise framework.' It was a view supported by many, including horror author Stephen King who added: 'What she said.'

Twitter's brand was modified because of consumer insight. But user behaviour didn't change that much, and the brand's proposition has been permanently compromised because it used to stand for 'really short messages' and now it stands for 'quite short messages'.

One year after the change, Slate published an article by Will Oremus titled 'Remember when longer tweets were the thing that was going to ruin Twitter?' He wrote,

At a time when Twitter is under scrutiny for its role in radicalizing right-wingers and fomenting anti-Semitism . . . and when CEO Jack Dorsey says he's rethinking everything: The anniversary of its character-limit change doubles as a reminder of a time when people didn't want Twitter to radically rearrange its core features.[17]

I'll tread carefully. Those working in HCD are close-knit and very vocal. Criticising the industry isn't done lightly, so here's some supporting evidence. Brent Smart is one of Australia's top marketers and former CEO of creative agency Saatchi & Saatchi. His marketing team won the annual Mumbrella Marketing Team of the Year award. Since becoming Chief Marketing Officer at insurance company IAG, he's been part of some incredible and highly effective brand-building work. In 2013, Smart said of customer journey mapping, a central tenet of HDC,

I don't think it delivers competitive advantage. It's hygiene ... When you focus on efficiency, you're able to show a commercial impact from marketing pretty quickly, but you're missing the bigger aspect of this conversation. Too many marketers focus on the efficiency side as opposed to the effectiveness side of things.[18]

Brands that apply HCD or customer journeys to increase efficiency and help consumers glide through their customer experience are building Teflon brands. They are not sticky, they are less memorable and they, therefore, reduce mental availability. This strips the value from the business.

A Teflon world

In 2018 *The New York Times* published a revealing article headlined 'How Amazon steers shoppers to its own products'.[19] It's worth a read if only to learn the difference between a monopoly and monopsony. In 2009 Amazon embraced the private label business and began offering unglamorous products such as batteries in its Home Basics category. Amazon's brand was available along with well-known battery brands Duracell and Energiser. When consumers run out of batteries, they don't ask Amazon's virtual assistant, Alexa, for more 'Duracells' or more 'Energisers'. They ask for more batteries. They care less about the brand and more about getting new batteries. The private-label batteries also happen to be 30 per cent cheaper.

Amazon told *The New York Times*, 'We take the same approach to private label as we do with anything here at Amazon: We start with the customer and work backwards.' Starting with the customer or customer experience is killing brands, because people don't need brands. They need the product. A company that puts the customer at the heart of its business can make brands redundant and, if not redundant, then generic.

Now bear with me as I become somewhat hyperbolic to make a point. When you watch a movie set in the future, the themes are similar. Everyone wears silver or red spandex, they have similar haircuts and they walk in unison. The lives of these futuristic people are depicted as seamless, frictionless (bloody HCD) and somewhat detached. There's often one mega-brand or company that controls everything. In *The Terminator*, it's Skynet. In Pixar's *WALL-E* (one of my top 100 movies of all time), mega-company Buy n Large controls everything from government to space travel to yoghurt. Science fiction takes an element of truth from today and imagines 'what if' in the future. In this world, brands disappear because the consumer doesn't need them. They need a product or service.

Following the imagination of science fiction writers, corporations are heading towards two outcomes. They will either be swept up to become a Buy n Large of their time — that is, fall into line with the business that controls everything. Or they will create something that's both different and distinctive — a brand with an idea. For the latter scenario to become a reality, a brand has to know what it stands for.

If you're in the whacky creative fringe, you might be nodding along saying, 'Darn right, the answers to life's questions are always in the movies'. But maybe you want to know what the science says.

We're already partly in a Teflon world

Consider the design of London's double-decker buses or Melbourne's trams. Both used to be ornate, with flourishes. Now both are streamlined and aerodynamically efficient human transport capsules lacking personality. Look at modern buildings: efficiency rules. We are already on the way to creating a *WALL-E*-like world: a super comfortable Teflon experience. Some of us want to challenge this and add some grit, cognitive disfluency and effort into the world we are designing.

Verda Alexander is responsible for designing many cool and fun workspaces. After designing many typical 'startup'-style workspaces with skateboard ramps, music rooms and in-house beer taps and baristas, she has since changed her focus and wants to design a workspace that is

. . . a little less comfortable and a little more challenging . . . Life is enriched by challenges. To face adversity, to labor is to be human . . . Friction gives us the ability to slow down, to focus, and to steer our attention where we want it to go..[20]

I love this approach. It reminds me of Building 20, which I read about in Steven Johnson's book *Where Good Ideas Come From*. Building 20 was a makeshift wooden structure built during World War II on the central campus of the Massachusetts Institute of Technology (MIT). The building was always considered temporary. When someone moved in, things were reconfigured, walls were bashed down or altered to fit their needs. The building was somewhat dilapidated and never 'perfectly' designed. It wasn't given a formal name or a dedicated purpose. But many unlikely meetings and unexpected conversations happened in Building 20 that led to the development of many new ideas. Several Nobel Prize winners worked there — especially in radar and nuclear physics. I discuss the importance of effort in chapter 5 when outlining the hope for stronger brands and businesses.

Many marketers are inadvertently creating Teflon brands. By listening to the consumer and giving them what they *think* they want, brands can slip in and out of consciousness. Being consumer-centric leads to brands and businesses that are only relevant when the consumer wants them to be. This isn't ideal. If you make things easier for them, be aware you may strip value from your business. The less they need to think about you, the worse it is.

Don't let this thought slide by

I hope I've convinced you that a consumer-centric approach will eradicate value from your brand and business. It leads to a lack of mental availability for your brand, meaning that when consumers have a need for you, you won't be there. This is a significant issue. It also devalues your brand because it doesn't reach people who rarely use the category. The bulk of sales are from people who rarely buy your brand. So unless you have non-stop advertising to the unengaged masses, there's little chance you'll pick them up. Further, if your product experience is seamless, it leaves a minimal impression in the mind for next time.

chapter 4
listening to the consumer makes your business homogeneous

When a consumer wants or needs a good or service, they don't think about the brand, but the category. If their car is always at the mechanics, they'll think about getting a new car, not a particular brand of car. If a family discovers their fridge isn't big enough, they'll think about buying a bigger fridge, rather than a particular brand of fridge. The category comes first, followed by the brand. The more you listen to the consumer, the more you understand the category. But if you're not careful, you begin to behave like everyone else in the category. It's the main reason so many brands within a category look and feel increasingly similar over time. Each brand draws on the same consumer needs and meets those needs in their respective brand offering. The more prolonged the existence of the category, and the longer the brand is within that category, the more homogenised it becomes.

Further, these days it's common to give everyone a say. Ideas are circulated for 'builds' and 'input'. But asking many people for input invariably leads to a regression towards the mean and ultimately, homogenisation.

Listen to Forrester. CX is dangerous

There's an unnecessary amount of attention given to customer experience (CX) and putting the customer first, and we see a massive homogenisation of brands already across many categories. Even those smart people at the international research agency Forrester agree. It's not an understatement to say they are a world leader in understanding technology and consumers and have tracked CX and its impact on branding for several years.

In a recent report, Forrester's principal analyst, Jay Pattisall, looked at the role of creativity in building brands and businesses and the role that consumer understanding has in limiting growth. He writes that CX 'has become homogenised, and technology is now table stakes as customers can no longer distinguish one experience from another'.[21] This should be pretty scary stuff for most brand owners — and I can demonstrate how prevalent the issue is right now. Go online and look at the landing pages of two or three of the big banks, or two or three fashion retailers, or the major supermarkets in your area. You'll begin to see how strikingly similar they are. It's the same when booking a flight regardless of the airline, or booking a room in a hotel. The CX for all of these brands within the same category is often the same and built off the same insights and consumer understanding. As the Forrester report describes, 'Every brand offered the same digital experience because they all address the same customer needs, use the same technology platforms, and design for the same mobile use case.'

Further, Forrester has measured CX for several years with its Customer Experience Index (CX Index™), based on proprietary consumer survey data. The CX Index shows little sign of brand progress. The implication is that brands are experiencing homogenisation because of CX-led solutions. Differentiation and bringing the brand to life is not happening because of the pursuit of CX. The CX Index goes to 100000 customers annually and is measured across 300 brands. In 2019, all 300 brands tracked by the CX Index were lapsing, lock-stepping or lagging. Digital sameness was pervasive. According to the report, organisations will have to look for a different way to grow their customer base. But before I continue with the heavy stuff, here's a fun anecdote about nappies.

Are you thinking of nappies?

In my book *The Advertising Effect: How to change behaviour*, I told the humbling story about the first time I bought nappies. Unfortunately for me, it wasn't for a baby. (That would happen in later years.) I was in Cannes about to give a keynote presentation in front of my advertising peers, but the night before the big event, I endured a horrific bout of diarrhoea. Rather than risk total humiliation, I bought a nappy and wore it under my jeans while on stage. It was a life-saver.

For most of us, nappies are one of the least cared about or considered products. We don't even think about them unless near the birth of a child. At that point, the care factor goes from zero to extremely interested rather quickly. This usually happens between the time your partner utters the words, 'Darling, I think it's coming' and 'Isn't he/she beautiful'. Just after the 'Isn't he/she beautiful' part comes the tender, cute but mildly disgusting and ultimately nerve-racking experience of putting a nappy on your child. It's a fiddly affair made all the more difficult by a black cord at the baby's belly button that has a big plastic peg clipped over the end of it. (You wonder if the peg should go in or out of the nappy.)

Anyway, the nappy is attached, the baby comes home and the parents then need to decide what brand of nappy to buy. They weigh up the pros and cons of up to three nappy brands, make their decision and then purchase the brand of nappy. If they, and the baby, have a positive experience with that brand, they'll probably repeat the purchase over the next four years. The example of nappies demonstrates the process by which most of us make decisions about brands. I'll take you through this model and explain why customer understanding is mostly responsible for the homogeneity of brands.

How we buy just about anything

In 2007, McKinsey consultants outlined the consumer decision journey. This replaced the linear sales funnel, first described by E. St Elmo Lewis in 1898 and regarded as the first formal theory of marketing. The sales funnel is an outdated concept that states consumers systematically move from awareness of your brand, through to discovery, evaluation, intent, purchase and loyalty. The problem with the funnel is the buying process is no longer linear. Prospects don't enter at the top of the funnel and steadily move through it. Instead, they enter at any point and may jump around the different stages or stay in one stage indefinitely. The loop captures a more complex decision-making process. My agency, Thinkerbell, uses a modified version of the purchase cycle when developing communications plans (see figure 4.1).

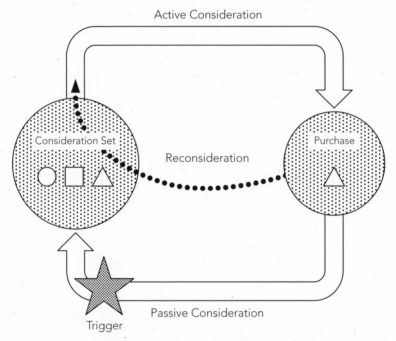

Figure 4.1: the purchase cycle for just about anything

Passive consideration

It all starts with passive consideration, a marketing euphemism that describes the state people are in when they're not thinking about your brand or business. In this stage, people go about their lives and don't care about your brand. They are oblivious to a brand's advertising and, if asked, would say they're not aware of it. This is where most consumers are most of the time. In the example of nappies, this is where people are until they reach the 'Isn't he/she beautiful' point. Most people don't care about nappies until there's a trigger: they're about to have a baby.

The trigger

The trigger happens when someone needs what your category offers. There can be several triggers for a particular category, known as 'category entry points', which I'll talk about later. In the case of nappies, the trigger is the birth of a child (or when giving a career-defining presentation in Cannes with a bout of crazy bad diarrhoea). If you are thirsty when entering a service station, you decide to buy a drink. The trigger is thirst. If your car fails to start, it triggers the thought that you should buy a new car. The birth of a child might also act as a trigger to buy a new car. A new job could trigger the need for a more impressive car. Importantly, the trigger is nearly always the category, not the brand.

The exception is when your business *is* the category, which is discussed in chapter 6. You need a drink, not a particular brand of drink. You need a car, not a specific brand of car. And yes, when you have a baby, you need nappies, not a particular brand of nappy. When the need for the category is triggered, then comes the realisation that several brands are available.

Active consideration

During this stage, each brand is considered and evaluated on how well it meets your wants and needs. Will this drink satisfy your thirst? Is the nappy adequately absorbent? The choice is assessed according to the consumer's goal for the category. The active consideration or evaluation process is complex and multifaceted, but I use this formula: what I get divided by what I pay times context. In the world of nappies, there are usually one to three brands to consider, and the job is to choose one brand.

Purchase/decision

After active consideration comes the decision. You choose a brand.

Reconsideration

After using the brand, you decide if you will use it again. Will you repeat this choice? If not, which brand will you choose next time? If you had a positive experience with a particular brand, you're possibly more likely to choose it again.

The consumer wants your category, not you

Now, you may be thinking, 'This is fine, Adam, but how does understanding the consumer make my brand generic?'

In chapter 3, I make a thought-provoking case that brand insight risks coating your brand in Teflon, where it slides in and out of consumer consciousness. The issue with the purchase cycle is that your brand is rarely considered in isolation; it's compared against alternatives. When a consumer is triggered to purchase, the category emerges and several brands come into consideration before the purchase. It's the job of each brand to stand for something distinctive and to occupy a unique place in a consumer's mind. When the category is triggered, your brand should own that real estate. However, the better a marketer understands the consumer, and the more they understand the triggers for the category, the more likely each brand will compete in the same category entry points using the same techniques, strategies, approaches and triggers.

Let me explain using a category I know a lot about: the hotel industry.

I'm sure you've had the experience of booking and staying at a business hotel. Most are pretty similar. Imagine your research asserts that price, location and comfort are the three strongest category drivers for choosing a business hotel. Other research reveals Instagram and morning TV influence consumer decisions. So you, along with most hotels, duke it out using these messages in these media environments.

A brand I'm familiar with has taken a different approach. QT Hotels is a chain of cool, upmarket hotels across Australia and New Zealand. Any time I visit Sydney, I insist on staying there. The hotel has several talking points — a fantastic bar, plush and sumptuous furnishings, free espresso martini makers in the rooms and the most incredible lifts. When you step into one of their lifts, the music is dynamically activated according to how many people are in the lift. If one person is in the lift, 'I'm so lonely' comes through the speakers. If two people are in the lift, you'll hear Dolly Parton and Kenny Rogers' singing 'Islands in the stream'. And if there are three or more people, it's party time. As popular and fun as it is, I doubt a consumer would include it on a decision tree matrix. It's merely a talkable feature of the hotel.

Steve Jobs said:

People don't know what they want until you show it to them. That's why I never rely on market research. Our task is to read things that are not yet on the page.

David Seargeant is cut from the same cloth. David is the founder and designer of QT Hotels, and he went beyond the predictable consumer triggers (price, location, comfort) to create a unique customer experience. He put BX (brand experience) before CX. For him, the brand expression is key. The brand expression is reflected in everything from the style of uniforms worn by reception staff to the eccentric in-house dining options to how guests are greeted to the look and feel of every room. Each is tightly controlled according to David's vision. Other hoteliers look at category drivers and drop the price of a room, talk about location and the excellent night's sleep you'll have at their hotel. And what does that lead to? Homogenisation. It's a real problem in the hotel industry as marketers focus on the guest over and above brand expression.

I worked with David on several campaigns for QT hotels. One of the most successful was 'Room for Dessert' around Valentine's Day. Diners at signature QT restaurants received an added surprise with their final course — a room key. When you ordered dessert, you were automatically checked into one of the designer QT rooms, with a half bottle of Champagne waiting for you (on ice, of course). As other corporate hotels dial up their location, comfy beds and proximity to the CBD, QT is creating its own rules.

A tension for most brands is a need to be part of the category when the consumer makes a decision. So, they each dial up the 'category drivers'. If market research finds the category drivers for hotels is comfy beds, then all hotels offer comfy beds. If people say they want a car that marries style with performance, that's what they'll all offer. The customer only considers what they need from the category, and brands clamber over one another to deliver on them – leaving differentiation by the wayside.

Homogenisation of style

Home furniture has also fallen victim to homogenisation, partly due to what I call the 'Pinterest-isation' of design. Discovered a lounge you love? Post it on Pinterest for others to like and share until all couches start to look the same. Design has been democratised, which isn't necessarily a good thing. As the mainstream grows, it's become more difficult for distinctive designers and lone wolf artisans to stand out. It's a gravitational power that's sucking everyone towards the norm.

Homogeneity within technology

Likewise, the logos of major technology companies reveal a determined stripping away of identity and individuality. According to type designer James Edmondson, brands have shifted from distinctive logos to ones with the same sans serif font. The 'o' in Spotify used to have three lines in rainbow formation above it, connoting sound. The letters in Airbnb were puffy with blue edging, suggesting a comfy bed in the sky. And Pinterest lost its craft look and its 'pin'. Perhaps the only logo that has improved is Google's, although its old one implied 'if we do a logo in colourful Times New Roman font it means we don't care about logos, which is possibly cool for a tech company like Google'. See figure 4.2 for the evolution of the logos over time.

So what happened? There are a few reasons for logo convergence. The newer logos are cleaner and easier to see on a small screen, which is what many of us use. Serif and curves are harder to view and messier on a small screen. But I think there's a richness in the mess, which I'll elaborate on later. Another reason is that tech startups generally can't afford slick, shiny logos when starting and a mate's mate does the job cheaply.

Figure 4.2: logo convergence

Source: Adapted from a tweet from OHnoTypeCo

Some brand experts suggest the logo isn't as important anymore. Who would confuse Google with Spotify? Ford makes trucks and McDonald's makes burgers, but both have identifiable logos. In my view, the scrappy edges, ugly bits and personality are being shaved off in our increasingly functional and utilitarian world. Logos are usually a mix of an ownable typeface with something of meaning to the company.

Over time, however, the logo is cleaned up and the rough bits removed. It means logos have become more generic and look like everyone else's in the category. Look at how the logos for AT&T and Google have changed over time (figure 4.3, overleaf).

Why do cars look like this?

There was a time not so long ago when different car brands looked, well, different. Today, if you removed the badge, many people wouldn't be able to identify the brand. This homogenisation is captured in designer Adrian Hanft's image of 23 cars from 21 manufacturers (figure 4.4, overleaf).

In his article titled 'The Zombie-mobile' Adrian says car manufacturers want to blend in rather than stand out. He writes,

> *Brand experts insist that success comes from promoting your unique attributes, but in practice, differentiation is less profitable than consolidation. In game theory, this is called the Nash equilibrium and is seen at every intersection where a Burger King opens across the street from McDonald's, or a Costco opens next door to a Sam's Club. Competition doesn't produce variety, it results in commoditization until we are left with 23 identical variations of the same vehicle.*[22]

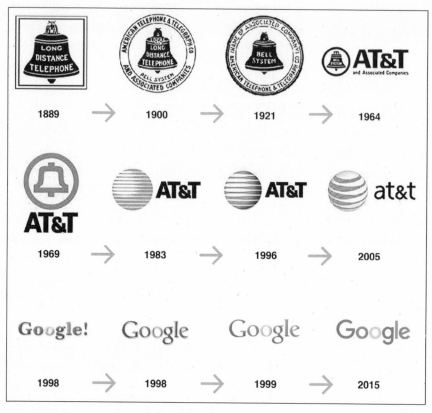

Figure 4.3: changing logos with the times

Figure 4.4: Adrian Hanft's 'Zombie-mobile'

Source: Adrian Hanft, *Medium*

He's right to some extent. It's much easier to conform and create a bigger category of sameness than stand for something different. However, this is precisely why listening to the consumer kills brands. Consumers don't want to think. They want things to be as easy as possible, and if you go along with that, it means offering the same product as everyone else, including cars. For example, before the advent of the SUV, every car manufacturer claimed their brand married style and performance. One of the few industry innovations was the development and demand for the SUV for perceived safety reasons. It's been a saviour for the car industry. Tesla is the only manufacturer to produce an entirely different car, and in 2018 it outsold Mercedes-Benz in the United States.

Tesla's approach to research

In chapter 6, I'll talk about how creating the category is a surefire way to ensure differentiation. In cases where your brand creates the category, any insights will be helpful because you are the only player in the category. This is the case for the Tesla Model X SUV, the first fully electric SUV alternative in the marketplace. Writing in Bloomberg, Dana Hull describes the process Tesla went through to make sure this car appealed to women, particularly so-called 'soccer moms'. Hull writes,

> ... Tesla invited a dozen women...for a three-hour focus group... The participants, most of whom drove minivans and SUVs, were asked what they like and don't like about their vehicles. Among the big issues: safety, a third row and getting kids in and out of car seats.

For a brand creating a new category, this is an excellent use of time, effort and money. The three-hour focus group uncovered the desires and gripes for a segment of consumers the organisation needed to understand. If the insights outlined in the article came from the focus group, it's great. But to be honest, I'm a bit sceptical because the insights that parents want safety, more space and easy access are hardly revolutionary. And Tesla delivered on them.

Marketing is a mass-market game

Some, but not all, agree with the notion that marketing is a mass-market game. Therefore marketers need to understand the drivers of the category that appeal to the most people and deliver on those drivers. As I mentioned before, if you're thirsty and want a bit of a pick-me-up you're likely to reach for a Coke (as it delivers on those drivers). Research companies have spent years attempting to understand category drivers. But the risk is the more you gain an insight into how consumers make decisions, and the more you act on this insight, the more likely it is you'll do what your competitors are doing, and therefore conform to category norms. In understanding the triggers for the category, you'll sell the brand at the same time and in the same way as the others. In understanding the category drivers, you'll risk building the brand and communicating in the same way as every other brand within the category.

Accounting firms all advertise the same message at the same time of year: 'We love numbers and tax knowledge even though you think it's boring'. Or take car brands, with their end-of-financial-year run-out sales — the categories act in unison, and everything starts to feel the same.

The wisdom of crowds also leads to homogeneity

James Surowiecki's best-selling book *The Wisdom of Crowds* had a significant impact on me. I was conducting a lot of market research at the time and it helped me see the value in what I was doing. When you speak with many people with diverse opinions and bring together their findings, you'll create something of value. The book also covers the ways in which market research often gets it wrong, and the conditions required to allow the wisdom of crowds.

The central premise of the book is that groups make better decisions than any single member of the group alone. The book opens with the story of a crowd at a county fair accurately guessing the weight of an ox when their guesses were averaged. Some speculated the ox to be heavier than it was, while others guessed it was lighter, while others guessed with greater accuracy. It stands that these guesses present themselves in somewhat of a normal distribution and the higher estimates counterbalanced the lower ones. In the end, the average is ascertained and that average is very similar to the ox's actual weight. It's an excellent example of the wisdom of crowds, or that 'none of us is as smart as all of us'.

The concept works in the case of guessing the weight of an ox or the number of jelly beans in a jar. It also arguably works with betting pools and predicting stock market rises and falls. Market research assumes that the same applies to ideas and brands. I think it has a similar effect, but that similar effect is damaging because it drags a brand towards the mean.

As mentioned earlier, most people assess a brand against how well the product or service meets the category need. And an array of insights, that is, the amalgamation of everyone's opinions, will invariably get you to a place where your brand services the mean.

In 2015, global professional services firm Ernst & Young made headlines around the world when it announced job applicants were no longer required to have a tertiary degree. The firm said it found no evidence of a positive correlation between academic success and achievement at the company, so they ditched the condition. This points to a growing lack of faith in the promise of tertiary education.

The tertiary education sector is very competitive, with universities fighting each other for students. Most conduct focus groups to gain an edge. It's something I know a bit about after conducting a series of them. One evening, I facilitated a group in a funky-looking room near the city. The vibe of the place was corporate cool, with deliberately mismatched furniture. It felt welcoming, except for the one-way mirror looming above the table and the microphones hanging low from the ceiling to capture every word. When I asked this group what they wanted from their university degree, one bohemian-looking woman said, 'People look at me and judge me, and on a bad day I judge myself too and think I'm just not ready to enter the workforce. What I want from university is both to feel ready to enter the workforce with the right skills, but more than that, I want to feel ready as an individual. I want to feel like I know what I need to know to get a job.' There were empathetic nods around the table.

Other people said they wanted to attend university to explore ideas and philosophy. One chap said, with a wry smile, that the primary purpose of going to university was to party as hard as you can because life will never be this easy again. Other people spoke about using the university as a testing ground to find out what they wanted to do. Another woman with shocking pink dreadlocked hair said university is a dream. She can lie on the lawn and daydream and then go and have coffee and talk about things. But the consensus view was that university would help them get a job. Ask many people what they want and it will come down to the average.

The university I did research for is competing against every other university. And guess what respondents said in their focus groups, surveys and questionnaires? They also said they want to get a job. And so over time, each university loses its identity and gravitates towards the mean. All promise that if you attend their university, you will get a job. The amalgamation of these insights, especially when you optimise the content through A/B testing, would look a little like figure 4.5, with the size of the bubble reflecting how many people agreed with that insight.

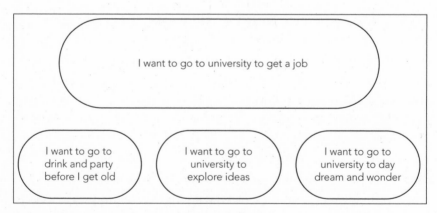

Figure 4.5: university focus group insights

It follows that most of the advertising in the category is against the biggest need, again leading to homogeneity. (I've called the institution 'Modern University' to protect its identity.)

Get Ready to Get A Job

If you attend Modern University, you'll learn everything you need to get a job. We'll prepare you well for your career so you will land a job with confidence.

Which university recommends the value of just letting your mind wander and be free? There are so many options available. I'm not saying any is right, and nor have I tested them to see which would be more effective. However, through research and opinion amalgamation, it's increasingly rare to see communications like this:

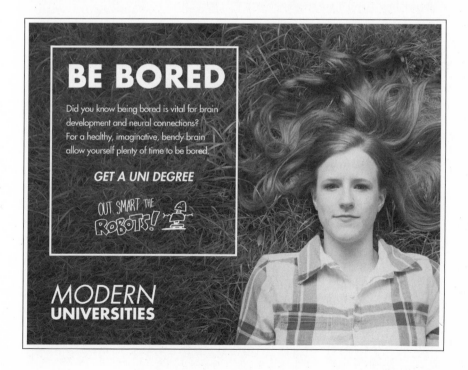

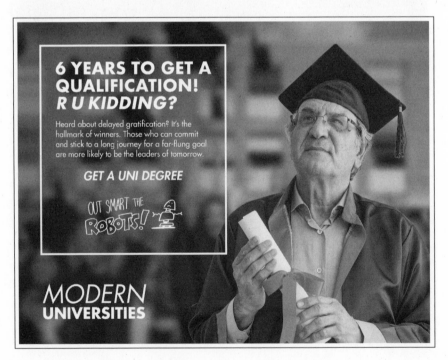

Each of these territories — imagination, broad learning, delayed gratification — are genuine and interesting to play with when considering what a university could stand for. But over time, there's a regression towards the mean because of the inundation of consumer insight.

There are several reasons why so many brands, especially older brands in mature categories, start to look and feel the same. But perhaps the main reason is they all draw on the same knowledge base. And this is a group of people who are all pretty much buying the same brands, and want precisely the same thing from each brand in the category. Unfortunately, not only does listening to the consumer make us more like everyone else, but it can also hamper breakthrough thinking.

Take the mock ads I created. They play with themes of exploration, boredom and the time taken to complete a degree. What does market research reveal about what people want from universities today? As well as an ability to get a job, prospective students asked for applied learning or study that's focused on real-world settings. They desire connections with the workforce and shorter, bite-sized courses. And it's in these areas that innovation is taking place with online education platforms such as Coursera, Udacity and MasterClass emerging. None is an established university. As a result, mainstream universities are now offering short courses, fewer arts subjects and more vocationally focused choices.

For some, this is great. I know of one university that's making excellent inroads in this space. But it's not the only option, and it becomes harder to notice other opportunities when you chase consumer insight at the expense of your brand.

This is not limited to education. Take another established category: banks. Most consumers say they want lower interest rates for lending products and higher interest rates for saving products. They want fewer fees and less complexity, and therefore that's what the major financial institutions all offer. The wisdom of crowds sometimes doesn't deliver a smart result.

What about Kodak?

Or any other brand that's no longer with us because it lost touch with what the consumer wanted and didn't adapt and remodel? Well, to those, I say, of course. I don't advocate keeping your head in the sand or suggest you ignore the consumer. I'm just trying to correct for the zealousness of a corporate culture that's chasing after every consumer insight. The other half of the marketing equation always has, and always will be, ensuring the consumer wants what you sell. We simply need to keep a balanced perspective. In order to stay ahead of the curve and innovate, it's important to understand where insights are from.

The difference between being customer led (bad) and understanding your market (good) was outlined in 1998 in an article titled 'Customer led, and market orientated: Let's not confuse the two' published in *Strategic Management Journal*.[23] Kodak, for the record, was neither; it was more 'head in the sand'. Understanding the latent, unexpressed and future needs of the market is preferable for an organisation (market orientation) rather than satisfying customers' expressed needs, which can be short-term, reactive and prioritised ahead of the brand.

Fear the power of tradition

A good friend of mine was pretty wild at university. He was always seeing bands, took loads of drugs and went off the rails. Fast forward ten years and he was an up-and-coming lawyer and settling down to get married. On the big day, he cut a fine figure in his suit. We were all shocked at how normal and textbook and lovely the wedding was. In his speech he said, 'Never underestimate the power of tradition', and I knew what he meant. We often fall into a groove or path because it's comfortable and familiar. This might work when choosing a life partner, but not in building a brand.

Brands need to stand for something distinctive. I hope I've highlighted the dangers inherent in asking groups of people about a brand or idea you may control. The more people you ask, the more the advice will take you to insights that already exist.

chapter 5
they who hear their brand

I've always liked the Warren Buffett quote, 'In the business world, the rear view mirror is always clearer than the windshield'. It perfectly sums up the dilemma most people in business face most days. We constantly make decisions about the future, not the past. And the future is always a little murky. It's much easier to look backwards or to gather data than it is to look forwards and have a stab. However, building a brand has as much to do with vision and clarity of thought as it does with art, science or experience. Some people are born with the skill of branding, while others develop it.

Here's a selection of people, brands and businesses that offer hope. The examples prioritise the brand and what the brand stands for above all else. I call this Brand Intelligence (BI; It's far superior to AI).

Hearing IKEA

Who would have imagined that a company started in 1943 by a Swedish carpenter, selling unpronounceable do-it-yourself products, would go on to become one of the most successful in the world? IKEA is synonymous with flat-pack, affordable furniture you construct yourself. But when you pull apart the IKEA consumer experience, you discover it breaks so many rules. IKEA is a classic case of a brand-led rather than consumer-led approach to marketing.

IKEA founder Ingvar Kamprad was obsessed with frugality. Even though he was one of the wealthiest people in the world, he always travelled in economy, drove an old Volvo and preferred discreet rather than overt displays of wealth. On one level, it was this Swedish utilitarianism that shaped IKEA's identity of functional design at an affordable price. As IKEA's former design manager Lars Engman summed it up, 'Sweden created the Volvo, Italy the Ferrari.' At a deeper level, Kamprad's vision weaves through the entire organisation. IKEA has been able to deliver low-cost design at the same time as steadfastly remaining true to its brand, rather than what a consumer might want. This includes a shopping experience that on the face of it is sub-par. IKEA's success is because of, not despite, the challenging shopping experience. Let me explain.

IKEA gets my vote for the least consumer-driven brand in the world. The Swedish behemoth seems to take pride in making the shopping experience as difficult as possible. Not only that, it forces consumers, after purchasing their products, to construct the items themselves.

Here is a typical user experience for an IKEA shopper:

1. A couple needs a child's desk and browses through an IKEA catalogue.

2. They decide to visit the nearest IKEA store, which is 45 minutes' drive from their house. Because it's the weekend, the place is crowded.

3. They park the car and enter the store. Once inside they are forced to follow a tightly defined route covering most of the warehouse-sized store. They see the desk they like and make a note of its number. They see other items they want, marking down the numbers.

4. After time in the store, they arrive at the collection area. In addition to finding and collecting their items, they make impulse purchases, claiming it will be a long time before they subject themselves to this nightmare again so they may as well stock up.

5. They look for assistance but can't find anyone, so sort it out for themselves using a tape measure, their hands and forearms.

6. They navigate an awkwardly loaded trolley of items to the cash register and pay.

7. They fill the car with flat-pack boxes and drive home.

8. When they finally arrive home, they unpack the car and start to construct the furniture. It doesn't quite match the other furniture in the house, but it wasn't expensive and will serve its purpose. The couple collapse on the couch with a glass of wine and gently rib each other about how crap they are at constructing IKEA furniture.

What was the total cost?

Desk

Desk	$400.00
Chair	$175.00
Lamp	$50.00
Rug	$120.00
Tea lights	$3.00
Total:	**$748.00**

How many hours did it take?

Viewing catalogue	30 minutes
Driving to the store	45 minutes
Time in store	90 minutes
Driving home	45 minutes
Unpack/build	90 minutes
Total:	**5 hours**

A customer-centric approach would be very different. This is the likely scenario:

1. A catalogue would only be available online. There would also be an option to purchase online.

2. There are several brick-and-mortar stores located around the city that are closer to more people and more accessible.

3. The website indicates if items are in stock. If unavailable, an alert will be sent by email.

4. Delivery would be available.

5. In the stores, there's no silly maze and people can walk however they like.

6. After finding an item in the store, a shopper tells the salesperson what they want. The order is put in and paid for. They don't have to go searching for it from a large warehouse shelf. It's delivered to their home.

7. The shoppers drive home.

8. The furniture is delivered already constructed or constructed on-site by the store staff.

What was the total cost?

Desk	$400.00
Chair	$175.00
Total:	**$575.00**

How many hours did it take?

Catalogue	30 minutes
Drive there	15 minutes
In-store	30 minutes
Drive home	15 minutes
Total:	**1.5 hours**

You can probably guess where I'm going with this. I hope it illustrates that a consumer-centric approach means less money and less time spent with the brand. And there's a difference you may not have picked up on. In the latter scenario, there's no glass of wine, no gentle ribbing and no experience. It might be much easier for the consumer, but, paradoxically, it offers less value to them.

How has IKEA been so successful despite, or because of, the shopping experience? It comes down to one word: effort. Consumers have to put effort into buying items at IKEA, and because of this they value the things more highly. Marketers and brand builders often talk about the need to reduce effort and to make things as easy as possible for the consumer. This thinking is not invalid. Removing friction and effort has led to increased profitability. However, the opposite is also true. We sometimes make choices precisely because they require effort.

The effort paradox

The insight that consumers feel rewarded from exerting effort would not have been uncovered by a researcher or from consumer mapping journey. IKEA – like Apple — will go down in history as the least consumer-centric brand in the world. The more difficult IKEA makes it for the consumer, the better it is for the brand. A research paper titled 'The Effort Paradox: Effort is both costly and valued' reveals that, contrary to the view that humans avoid tasks that involve effort, the opposite is also true. Effort can add value. 'Not only can the same outcomes be more rewarding if we apply more (not less) effort, sometimes we select options precisely because they require effort.'[24] IKEA pushes many of these effort triggers, including:

- cognitive dissonance and error justification
- need for cognition
- sunk cost effect
- the IKEA effect
- learned industriousness.

Effort justification

When we put effort into something, we justify this action by finding the experience itself rewarding. For example, if we spend an entire morning at IKEA and come home with a bookcase, we'll say it was rewarding to support the time spent on the task.

Need for cognition

Many people enjoy a cognitive activity such as problem-solving. Staff at IKEA are trained to leave customers alone and allow us to work it out for ourselves. They won't approach as you measure an item or try to make the boxes fit on your trolley. They know that deep down, you secretly love trying to work it all out yourself.[25]

Sunk cost effect

People are more likely to continue pursuing something if energy and effort have already been invested in obtaining it. For example, if you spend an hour walking around the IKEA store, you've sunk an hour into the trip. You'll then sink more money into the trip by buying more stuff to justify your time at IKEA. When was the last time you walked away from IKEA with nothing? It rarely happens, because of the sunk cost effect.

The IKEA effect

This was theorised by Harvard Business School Professor Michael Norton. People place a higher value on products they successfully build or prepare themselves than identical products that are ready-made or made by others. What happens after you've constructed that bookcase? You value it approximately 30 per cent more than if it arrived ready made.[26]

Learned industriousness

People's reward for putting in the more significant effort is a positive sensation from this effort. We discover that putting effort into a task feels good and we seek out that feeling again. We head back to IKEA even though we swore we'd never go there again.

Following the death of Ingvar Kamprad, I'm concerned about the direction of the company. I think it's losing its way. The company has introduced several changes that make it easier for the consumer to shop with them. One difference is a click and collect service. There is also a partnership with a company that will deliver, build and install the furniture for you. Finally, smaller, easier-to-access stores are opening. These changes suggest the company is listening to the customer, which I think is a big mistake.

What about Apple?

Some companies don't rely on research. Nike is one. Apple is another. As Apple's co-founder Steve Jobs said in *Businessweek* in 1998, 'It's really hard to design products by focus groups. A lot of times, people don't know what they want until you show it to them.' Many of us believed Apple didn't conduct market research and instead relied on the creativity of its designers and the omnipresent strength of its brand. But it would appear Apple's relationship with research is more complicated. In 2012, Apple had a legal battle with Samsung and Apple's VP of Product Marketing argued its research should be exempt from the hearings. The claim was unsuccessful and the world discovered Apple *did* do market research, although it was less traditional (focus groups) and more usability focused (observational). Yet Apple is still a flag-waving champion for a company that puts its brand and brand experience ahead of the consumer wants or needs.

Consider the long list of product irritations initiated by Apple:

- ◆ Consumers hate it when products quickly become out of date or break down, and they have to purchase a new one. Even worse is planned obsolescence, where the manufacturer deliberately plans for a product to become obsolete. This practise is illegal in many countries. Yet has anyone noticed their phone slowing down following a so-called 'upgrade'?

- ◆ The cords, dongles and power adapters continuously change. Anyone with an Apple product has to have a bag full of obsolete dongles and cables.

- ◆ The system steadfastly rejects or operates poorly with non-Apple accessories.

- Apple products, especially the iPhone, are expensive compared to near-identical competitors.

- The repairs are expensive, and so too are the accessories: like, really expensive.

There are other annoyances, but these are enough to do me for now. Of course, I've typed this list on a MacBook Pro (which often displays the wheel of death). If Apple put the consumer ahead of the brand, many of these long-standing issues would have been resolved years ago. But would the brand be better for it?

Tourism Australia

It started with a teaser that looked like an official film trailer. As the camera pans along what appears to be a gorge in outback Australia, the words, 'The Son of an Australian Legend Returns Home' are projected on the screen. Standing above the gorge on a red rock is a man dressed like the original Crocodile Dundee. He says 'Good-day, losers' in an American accent. There's Chris Hemsworth, Margot Robbie, Hugh Jackman, Liam Hemsworth, Isla Fisher, Russell Crowe, Ruby Rose and Jessica Mauboy. The spot finished with 'Summer 2018 #dundeemovie' on the screen. Social media erupted: was Crocodile Dundee 4 coming to the big screen? If not, then what? The question was answered on 5 February 2018 during the world's most-watched ad break: the Super Bowl. The teaser was a fake and an ad for Tourism Australia. It screened in front of a potential 110 million viewers, making it the boldest campaign ever seen in the tourism sector and winning numerous advertising awards. The campaign has been extremely successful, with bookings up by 13 per cent and intention to book up 83 per cent.[27]

The campaign didn't end there. My agency created a sequel to the ad with the express aim of converting interest in visiting Australia to buying a plane ticket. The sequel, 'Come Visit the Set of Dundee', was born. It starred the lesser-known, 'original' Hemsworth, Luke Hemsworth, treating Australia as one big studio back lot. As he drives a golf buggy down a red dirt road, the jewels in Australia's tourism crown are on display, from the Barrier Reef, Ningaloo Reef, Sydney Harbour VIVID and Freycinet in Tassie to the cube building in McLare South Australia.[28]

We presented our pitch to then Chief Marketing Officer of Tourisn. Australia, Lisa Ronson. She estimated the entire campaign would add $860 million to the Australian economy by 2020. I think the campaign also reaffirmed Australia's identity as self-deprecating and casual. We don't take ourselves too seriously and offer light-hearted relief captured in the character of Mick Dundee.

In 2018, Lisa was ranked number one on the CMO50, a list that recognises Australia's innovative and effective marketing leaders. I asked for her general views on research for brands and marketing campaigns and whether she relied on consumer research to help decide on an idea, or improve it. She said she isn't an advocate of creativity by committee. If you are clear about the problem to solve, the outcome and what the brand stands for, these filters help to determine the best idea.

How did Lisa know she was backing the best idea in our Dundee pitch? She told me the idea was simple, smart and compelling. Luke Hemsworth's ability to have a joke at his own expense sums up Australians, and she liked the idea of extending on the Super Bowl ad by turning Australia into a movie set. Research helps if you have a problem to solve. A great creative idea isn't a problem that needs to be solved.

This is where getting the foundations right is critical; otherwise you will be 'spraying and praying' with your brand. The foundations are your vision, your purpose — why you get out of bed every day beyond making money — your brand personality and values. Also having a very clear understanding of what aspects of your brand need work to ladder up to your vision and purpose. This provides a good lens for what you do as well as what you don't. The key is in recognising and backing brave, creative ideas that will really shift the dial in brand fame, consumer engagement and drive business outcomes. As a marketing community, we have become far too safe and don't back ourselves. To link to the previous question, market research often compounds this problem.

I agree with her about strong foundations, including a clear understanding of what your brand stands for and where it is heading. Once these are in place, you can then unleash creativity.

A bit of romance

In a world that's chasing efficiency (and creating homogenisation), I'm observing a counter-trend in some corporate offices. There's a yearning for the irrational, the beautiful and, dare I say, romantic. A friend and PR guru Catherine King formed an agency with a bunch of collective misfits called The Romantics. She believes smart divergent people need to come together to solve problems. But problems are not addressed in a board room or a workshop environment. Cath takes them into a romantic setting and explores the romance of the problem.

Cath would get on well with Tim Leberecht, author of *The Business Romantic*. Tim believes the world has chased efficiency for long enough. Thanks to persuasive technologies, big data and a desire to measure and quantify everything, we've almost eaten the final crumbs of the efficiency pie. We can keep trying to dial up the efficiency but, just like promising lower prices, it's ultimately a promise to nowhere. As Tim says,

> *We can no longer afford efficiency. To be fair, efficiency once served us well. It was the engine behind the industrial age, and as we have been shifting to the post-industrial one, it has helped us squeeze the last drop out of a tightening system. But with top-line growth becoming paramount for most businesses, it is time to acknowledge that efficiency alone is producing diminishing returns.*[29]

Tim explains why efficiency is potentially so dangerous. In my world, efficiency is based on consumer understanding — of understanding consumers at every turn and giving them precisely what they need. If we make things as easy as possible for consumers to get what they want, we end up in a 100 per cent efficiency wasteland. As depicted in *WALL-E*, everyone is overweight, wearing the same clothes and getting around in personal jet-propelled mini-cars. They never need to move and everything is brought to them. A perfectly efficient future ends up disabling humans and hindering their creativity. According to IKEA, *Wall-E*, and Cath and Tim, efficiency is the end of the line.

It's a mistake to chase efficiency. Efficiency means call centre staff are rewarded for dismissing problems as quickly as possible. It creates chatbots so even fewer staff are needed. Chatbots are not the answer. Our client 13cabs represents the majority of the taxi industry in Australia. One of its competitive advantages is a call centre for those who don't want to book a cab through an app. Some callers are elderly, confused or have special needs. The staff who answer these calls have the time to assist them. In fact, some of the ads we created for 13cabs featured actual calls to the company, the content is that powerful.

Efficiency doesn't tolerate waste or fantastic ideas, and is the enemy of creativity and innovation. Efficiency optimises what already exists. In focusing on what already is and improving on it, you miss opportunities to create something better. It's unfortunate that in a world where everything can be measured, we focus on the measurable. We can measure our five senses, and we can deliver on this. However, it's still tough to measure what happens in our hearts and our feelings. And this brings me to romance. Romance is the enemy of efficiency.

Romance, almost by implication, means chasing the irrational. Romance is the relaunch of a Volkswagen Beetle with a flower on the dashboard. Romance is Google changing their logo every once in a while with a new Google Doodle. Heck, romance is IKEA recognising you enjoy Saturday morning even more if you build a bookcase yourself rather than have it delivered ready made. If you asked a consumer if they were more inclined to buy a car because it had a pink flower on the dashboard, the answer would be no. If you asked a consumer if they would pay more for a bookcase they had to assemble themselves, the answer would be no. Focusing on the consumer leads to efficiency. Concentrating on your brand offers the scope for innovation, expression and the ability to surprise and delight.

Art Series Hotels

Quentin Tarantino has Uma Thurman; I have Art Series Hotels. I've worked with them for years and they are a favourite client because they know their brand so well. With limited budgets but great brand understanding, we've been inspired to create big ideas with mainly outrageous success. In fact the Art Series Hotel chain was sold last year for squillions, and one of the reasons the sales price was so high was how Art Series Hotels advertised; they know their brand. As their agency partner, I just delivered on a very clearly articulated central organising thought of 'art-inspired experiences' that met the tone of the brand. The ideas we've done together include:

◆ *Steal Banksy*. This was the first idea and involved inviting people to 'stay the night and steal the art'. In the hotel, a piece of Banksy art was hung on the wall. If a guest was able to steal it, they could keep it. If they were caught, the art was returned to the wall. It was eventually stolen in a well-constructed heist. The campaign won a gold Lion at Cannes and a Gold Effie for effectiveness.

◆ *Overstay checkout*. Overstay, you're welcome. Every morning guests could ring up and see if anyone had booked the room that night. If not, they could keep staying there for free. In fact, they could stay for free until the room was next booked. The guests felt so good about the deal, they spent money at the hotel's bar and restaurant. It's been so successful, the hotel has run the promotion for several years. The idea won a Silver Lion, a Gold Effie, WARC World of Innovation Award and Retail Innovation of the Year.

◆ *Which Warhol*. We would hang a real Warhol with a number of fakes. If someone guessed the right one, they could keep it. (We had bad legal advice here and had to terminate the promotion with an apology.)

- *Reverse reviews.* Instead of the guests reviewing the hotel, the hotel reviewed every guest. This idea was bold and audacious and won several awards and earned media from around the world.

- *Art in micro.* We conducted a micro art exhibition and invited people to stay the night and find the art. The campaign took place with plenty of earned media.

Here's the press release from the Art in Micro launch, the latest (although I'm sure not the last) idea.

Art Series Hotels and Thinkerbell launch something very small.

This weekend, Art Series Hotels launches 'Art in Micro', an exhibition of micro art—the next big thing in the art world. Guests will be given the opportunity to win a trip for two to Le Louvre, Paris, during their stay. On check-in they'll be handed a magnifying glass, along with a catalogue of the artwork and prompted to find every micro art piece—some of which may prove to be all too tricky to see with just the naked eye. Art Series Hotels' Marketing Director Ryan Tuckerman says 'We have a rich history of supporting and exploring contemporary art forms, and believe micro art will be of particular fascination this exhibition season.'

'Across the eight of our Art Series Hotels, over 40 pieces of micro art have either been purchased directly from artists around the world, or have been loaned', Tuckerman says. The exhibition features artwork such as sculpted pencil leads by Salavat Fidai, the ceramic miniatures of Jon Almeda, micro dioramas of urban decay from Joshua Smith and micro watercolour on canvas by Varvara Razakova. 'It's amazing how something so small can have such an impact; everyone on the project has been in absolute awe of the level of detail these artists go to with their craft', says Adam Ferrier from Thinkerbell. For more information about Arts Series Hotels, visit www.artserieshotels.com.au/artinmicro/.

Along came ALDI

Occasionally (well, quite often) I see an ad campaign that I wish our agency had devised and implemented. One example is the great and continuing work for the discount supermarket chain ALDI. The first time you walk into an ALDI store it's somewhat disorientating. You might find a lawnmower placed next to a container of biscuits by brands you don't know but that look familiar to the ones you usually buy. This is a key component of ALDI's success — in-house brands that look like existing brands but at discount prices. As the company says,

> From the beginning, ALDI stood out from the rest of the supermarket pack. . . . Our products were unfamiliar to the Australian public. And customers were asked to pack their own bags. It didn't take long for Aussies to recognise these differences for what they were — a commitment to saving shoppers money.[30]

But not everyone was convinced. And in 2015, ALDI Australia ran the 'Supermarket Switch Challenge' (created by BMF Advertising) that aimed to convert so-called ALDI sceptics. These were shoppers turned off by the store's quirkiness and unfamiliarity. 'It's just so random,' says one guy. The campaign recruited fans of the store to convince their sceptical friends to make the switch. The sceptics discovered that even though there were brands they didn't recognise, some of their favourites, such as Vegemite, were on the shelves and at lower prices. One woman says of the store layout, 'It's bigger than I expected.' As a result of the campaign, 661 000 new households started shopping at ALDI.

Hear the brand

As these stories show, it doesn't matter what type of business it is; any organisation can understand and live by its brand. In my experience, the commercial sector generally defines its brand in a clear and readily understood way. That's not to say there aren't great examples in the not-for-profit and charity sector as well. You can be brilliant at hearing, defining and disseminating what a brand stands for regardless of the offering.

Hearing what the brand means and ensuring it's clearly communicated is perhaps Marketing 101, but it's become more difficult to hear the brand because of the noise created by consumer research and behavioural data. As these examples have shown, there are many great brands that do a brilliant job of it.

chapter 6
create the category

The dream for a business is to operate as a monopoly. If you operate as a monopoly within a category that enjoys healthy consumer awareness and demand, the business will thrive. One of the founders of PayPal, Peter Thiel, outlines this aspiration in *Zero to One*. The theme of the book (and the author's life) is that entrepreneurs should attempt to create an entirely new category rather than compete with an existing brand in a category. It should go from zero to one. If you are the one, you have created a category of one.

The ability to create a new category is rare, but the benefits are enormous. If you ever find yourself in this position, you need to ride it hard and fast because, without a doubt, competitors will come along and breathe down your neck. Let me describe the experience of my mate and former colleague, Rob Perkins, who managed to achieve this feat.

Making sex better

Before he became a Silicon Valley multimillionaire, Rob Perkins worked for me at Naked Communications. Rob is highly charismatic, creative and curious. Before becoming an entrepreneur, he produced some of the world's best-known and most successful advertising campaigns. Rob loves ideas, has a passion for pushing boundaries and is always willing to intellectually go where others do not. This predisposition may have been encouraged in childhood; he is the son of a psychiatrist, as it happens. Rob reckons interesting people have generally been in therapy. It means they're more comfortable talking about uncomfortable subjects.

One of Rob's observations was around sex and the degradation resulting from porn culture. Porn used to consist of a *Playboy* centrefold passed around the schoolyard, but now there's a cornucopia of content a click away on the internet. The volume of porn has exploded. Unfortunately for young people, pornography is used as a surrogate sex educator. Many believe their partners will want sex in the way it's depicted in porn. Most partners don't.

Rob observed that sex education hasn't kept up with modern mores and is rather embarrassing and irrelevant. Because it's taught in a classroom, an in-depth discussion is mostly absent.

Rob has always believed in Peter Thiel's advice about innovation at a category level rather than at a brand level. If you innovate at a category level, you can achieve something more profound and disruptive. Creating an entirely new category allows you to have significantly more influence and interest, whereas creating a new brand within a category is just a fight for market share.

So Rob created the website OMGyes.com — the Science of Women's Pleasure, a series of online interactive instructional videos to make sex education shameless, open and effective. Actress Emma Watson revealed she subscribes to the site. And after reading this, you might sign up as well.

Rather than risk misrepresenting Rob and his achievements, I went straight to the source and asked him to describe OMGyes.com in his own words. Here's my chat with Rob and a demonstration of his brilliant brain.

Adam: How did OMGyes.com start?

Rob: It started as just a fun project — we'd ask our circle of friends to share their insights about specific techniques and the sexual pleasure discoveries they wish they'd known about sooner. And then we'd look for the patterns. You'd think this request to share would be met with raised eyebrows and different variations of 'no thanks', but everyone wanted to be involved. The project grew fast, and we realised something in culture was changing. People were hungry to talk openly about this stuff and to understand it better. We did a bunch of thought experiments — and one was to imagine a future without the taboo, where this new openness and honesty we were seeing had grown and grown, breaking like a giant wave over all the cultures in the world. What would have to happen to get to that version of the future? And we realised these interviews, themselves, were transformative — not just for the person sharing, but for us, the interviewers. And if the world could see interviews just like these, this particular kind of openness would be contagious. After the initial giggles, with no-one cringing or uncomfortably changing the subject, it becomes obvious that hearing about the specific kinds of touch people like with their partners (or by themselves) is fascinating. And when you see it, from relatable people of widely different ages, it becomes clear: that's how it should be. The sky doesn't fall. No-one's trying to arouse anyone else in the conversation. There's laughter, but it's good, healthy, 'I didn't know it, but I've been waiting for someone else to say that' laughter.

In doing what turned into over a thousand interviews, we discovered not just the patterns in sexual pleasure techniques, but also a lot about the taboo. We learned about the rampant myths and misconceptions that are going unquestioned because of the silence surrounding the topic.

Adam: Why does innovation best happen at a category level and why is it not generally born out of customer insight?

Rob: We're big believers in the blue ocean strategy notion. That there are lots of red ocean areas where there are already lots of sharks (companies) competing and copying each other. And there are also lots of completely blue ocean areas — where no-one is yet. When building products in blue ocean, there aren't standard features or ways of behaving. You're making it up as you go along and picking and choosing some approaches from other categories.

So we learned early on when we talked to potential customers that we couldn't rely on them to tell us what to build. Because their framework for what was out there and possible didn't include products like ours. When we showed them the product, that's when the light bulb went on, and they'd try to make sense of it. That was really valuable research — understanding how people would explain this new thing to their friends.

OMGyes is my favourite example of a brand creating the category. There's still nothing like it.

Bending an established category into a new shape

It's more common for a category to be disrupted and bent into a different shape than for a whole new category to be invented. As mentioned earlier, there's barely any brand differentiation between Australia's big four banks because the category has existed for a long time, as have the banks.

The eruption of financial technology (fin-tech) companies offering mobile-first banks is expected to challenge this. If one or two disruptive companies develop something completely new, it will bend the banking sector into a new shape. If my theory holds, they will also attract new customers. The bank that bends the category will attract attention and customers.

Using advertising to dent the category

I know Apple keeps on popping up in this book. Apologies if you're not into its ecosystem. But what's noteworthy about Apple is it didn't create a new category, it just put a considerable dent in a category that already existed. Before Apple came along, personal computers were marketed to nerds. Then along came Apple, the nerd barrier was knocked over and personal computing became cool. The company achieved this through slick product design and an advertising campaign that reinforced that story.

In 2010, *Adweek* declared 'Get a Mac' to be the best advertising campaign during the first decade of the new century. Its evolution had Steve Jobs's fingerprints all over them. There were tantrums and rejections, with thousands of scripts tossed out for the smallest of reasons. More than 200 ads were made, but only 66 made it to air. The campaign ran from May 2006 to October 2009 and used two actors to represent a Macintosh computer and Microsoft Windows PC. Within these ads, the Mac and PC were friendly, but different. PC is nervous and fidgety, prone to breaking down and getting viruses. The actor wears an uncomfortable-looking business suit. Mac is cool and casual and seems much more relaxed in his jeans, sneakers and a comfy t-shirt.

This remarkably simple campaign helped Apple push the category in a new direction. Personal computing didn't need to be complicated, confusing and boring. Those who didn't view themselves as geeks but part of the creative class felt more comfortable with a Mac made by Apple. Even though the Mac and PC have similar functionality, this campaign focused on smart differentiation, which led to an attitudinal change towards the category because now a 'cool' computer was available to purchase.

Taxi please

According to Uber, 'On a snowy evening in Paris, Travis Kalanick and Garrett Camp can't get a cab — the idea for Uber is born'. As they wait in the cold, they wish there was an app that could order a chauffeur-driven car to pick them up. Fast forward not too many years later and Uber is ubiquitous. It married two categories — the accessible taxi and the high-end chauffeur. The idea didn't come from studying the behaviour of consumers. It happened because someone had the great idea of merging the convenience of taxis with the luxury of private hire cars. By securing the category and owning it, Uber could then focus on the customer experience.

It has clearly created the category of ride sharing. In many markets they are (or were) operating as a monopoly, so any customer insights were now not generic, but actually aimed at helping to build the Uber brand. Uber found several pain points for consumers and removed them such as booking the car (via the app), wondering if it will arrive (via driver ratings), wondering when it will arrive (via watching the car come to your home), wondering if it's your car (via number plate and colour matching), ensuring the driver knows where you're going (plugging in details before you get in the car), paying at the destination (via paying over the app). These are small yet significant changes that make it easier for the consumer to do their thing. However, Uber is now in a world of pain. A *New York Times* article, 'How Uber Got Lost', describes how pushback against the exploitation of drivers, an inability to invest back into the company and negative corporate reputation are contributing to a company that is yet to make a profit.[31] And at this stage, it looks like it never will.

The mandatory paragraphs on Tesla

In 2006, I watched a fantastic documentary about the fate of the battery electric vehicle in the United States. It's called *Who Killed the Electric Car?* and it argued that thanks to lobbying by the car industry, electric cars were unable to crack into the US car market. It was a captivating documentary, but unfortunately for them, it dated very quickly. Soon after the film screened at the Sundance Film Festival, director Chris Paine announced he was working on a new movie with the working title *Who Saved the Electric Car?* It was later called *Revenge of the Electric Car*, starring Tesla's Elon Musk. Tesla is an interesting organisation because, like Uber and Apple, it hasn't changed the product but still managed to put a dent in the category. Peter Thiel writes about it in detail in *Zero to One* (the two were business partners at PayPal). Musk has gone to great lengths to downplay the differences between his electric vehicles and traditional cars. The only difference is that Tesla is powered by a lithium-ion battery pack rather than a combustible engine.

Musk has packed the Tesla with car-like features. The vehicles can reach high speeds, going from zero to 100 quicker than any other passenger car in history, and the 'falcon wing' doors look cool. These features make Tesla a viable alternative and negate the perceived risks that could be associated with the purchase of an electric car. Rather than establish electric cars as a category, Musk successfully put a dent in the car category with electric vehicles. Other Tesla innovations include owning the dealer network and selling directly to the consumer. And in creating electric cars with top line technology, other electric car manufacturers are benefitting. He's made electric cars look bloody cool. As other companies enter the category, Musk will hope his temporary monopoly has given him the competitive edge needed to win the race for the electric car.

Stretching a pre-existing brand

I've said it before, and I'll say it again: creating the category is hard. But if you're innovative, that's where you should put your focus. At their heart, brands are 'emotional', and this emotion allows them to stretch into all sorts of areas. It's why several serial entrepreneurs take their brands from business to business. For example, Netflix shifted from a DVD postal service to a DVD and Blu-ray rental business, to a streaming business, and finally a content creation company — all called Netflix. Sir Richard Branson's Virgin brand has always positioned itself as 'the consumer champion'. An emotive promise can be parlayed into categories as diverse as airlines, music, bridal wear, gyms, finance and even to mobile phone plans.

If you work with a sizable pre-existing brand, I suggest you stretch the brand into a new category rather than starting another brand to match the opportunity. Brands often have far more stretch in them than people believe.

Be the category

Where possible, be the category. But the next best thing is to put a dent in an existing category. My tip is this: you won't create a category by asking consumers what they want. As Rob Perkins explained, potential customers couldn't tell him what product or experience to create because their framework didn't include products like his. Peter Thiel believes there are still unchartered frontiers to explore and new inventions to create. And if you crack any of those nuts, enjoy the ride.

If you're out in front in a category of one - enjoy it for as long as you can. Others will mimmick, copy, and be derivitive off your success. However, if you're first you have the opportunity to scale and have complete market share — and that's a great place to start.

chapter 7
define the brand

You're about to read the most practical chapter in this book. After perusing it, you'll know the precise steps involved in creating a brand. I can tell you now, the process is simple — but it's in the execution where it becomes difficult. The information is based on my experience with brands I've created and brands I've worked on.

A brand I'm particularly proud of

I love working in marketing sciences. I also enjoy consulting and helping businesses build their brands. During consults I'm sometimes asked, 'What would you do if it was your money?' and 'You're good at giving advice but have you a brand yourself?' The answer is yes. I've created several business brands, written a book, created a board game and developed a couple of conferences. But nothing gives me greater pride than defining and co-creating with my partners my latest company, Thinkerbell.

The main difference when defining a brand for yourself rather than a large organisation is fewer stakeholders. Negotiations only had to happen with my business partners. We met when working as minor partners at the same agency. It wasn't the right fit for us, so we left and started a new agency. We roughly knew the services we would offer, which happened to match our skill set, but that's all we knew.

What's the category?

The first thing we did was look at the marketplace and understand the category we were entering. It's no secret that the traditional advertising market is declining, but the consulting world is growing. Just look at the share prices of creative transformation company WPP, and multinational professional services company Accenture. We wanted a brand and business that could straddle both worlds. My previous experience at Naked Communications taught me it's important to be different but also easy for people to be able to buy you. Naked was very different, but we were also not really an agency like the others and therefore potential clients had trouble knowing when to buy us, or use our services. We didn't want to create an entirely new category but did want to bend the shape of what an agency could be in today's complex marketing landscape.

What's our promise?

Next up, we needed to articulate our brand promise or central organising thought. To work this out, we wondered what made us different from other agencies, what was motivating to prospective clients and what was true to the business and to the three of us (although we soon after took on another partner, Margie, as well as an investment from PwC). I'm a psychologist/marketing sciences/strategist with a creative bent. 'Cuz' is an art director with an artist's soul. And Jim is a through-and-through problem solver. After some deliberation, we decided we represented 'marketing sciences meets hardcore creativity'. We liked this broad thought as it also helped to reconcile what our clients grapple with: many different options and opportunities. The range of marketing options has exploded at the same time as budgets are reducing, stakeholders are growing in number and there's greater accountability for every dollar spent. The 'marketing sciences meets hardcore creativity' proposition helps clients reconcile this fundamental tradeoff in the category — there's both increased opportunity and increased accountability.

To make the message stick, we needed a more straightforward way of expressing our central idea and came up with two alternatives: 'controlled creativity' or 'measured magic'. After a little discussion, 'measured magic' won. Measured magic is our promise, delivery and central organising thought, and this will never change.

How do we deliver?

A brand requires more than a central organising thought. We had to offer reasons to believe we could deliver on 'measured magic' and developed three key ways we'd deliver on the promise.

Four-leaf clover

The first reason to believe we can deliver on measured magic is our thoroughly considered 'Four-leaf clover' process (see figure 7.1).

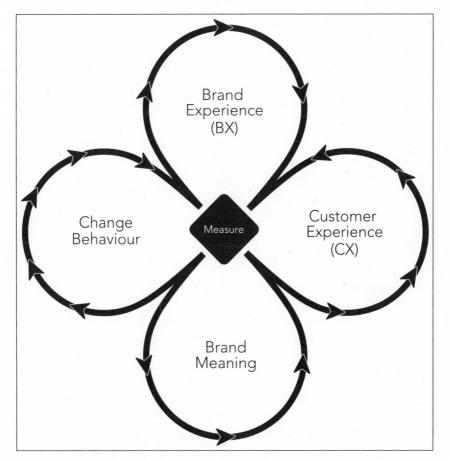

Figure 7.1: our four-leaf clover

A four-leaf clover is rare and meant to bring good luck. Two of the leaves represent 'brand thinking', and two represent 'consumer thinking' — in that order.

Let me run through the brand thinking represented in figure 7.1 with a real-life example. Sukin is Australia's biggest natural skincare brand and famous for pioneering 'the no list' — a list of ingredients their products don't include. We suggested amplifying the no list because it was a strong and distinctive asset. Here's the process:

♦ *Leaf 1: Brand Meaning.* What does the brand stand for? We distilled Sukin's brand essence to be: 'it's what we leave out that makes us special'.

♦ *Leaf 2: Brand Experience (BX).* This is the consumer-facing articulation of what the brand wants to stand for. This idea is summarised in a brand book with style guide recommendations. For Sukin this came to life with the line 'Nothing but special' (see figure 7.2). The communications were stripped back, minimal and beautiful.

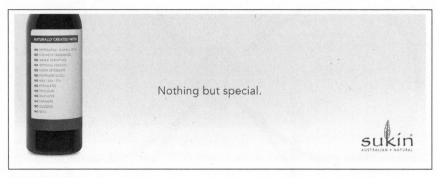

Figure 7.2: a billboard for the Sukin 'Nothing but special' advertising

♦ *Leaf 3: Change behaviour.* Once a brand is in place, we want to understand how we can use the brand to change behaviour. We look at the consumer, what they are doing and what we want them to do. For Sukin, this means taking all of the brand expression work, the look and feel of the brand, the distinctive brand assets we've created (such as 'the no list' and the simplicity of communications, as well as the green and cream colour palette) and using these to create advertising and communications that change behaviour and encourage people to try the brand.

◆ *Leaf 4: Customer Experience (CX).* This leaf is dedicated to understanding how we can continue to build the brand experience for the consumer, so they stick with us and build a relationship with the brand. We offer content, ideas and conversation with Sukin consumers to keep them involved in the brand. For example, we asked them to provide content for a large user-generated campaign. In chapter 12, I describe how to get people to invest in a brand so they value it more.

Thinkers and Tinkers

The second reason to believe in our agency promise of measured magic is our 'Thinker and Tinker' business model. Everyone is either a Thinker or a Tinker. Our topline description of each of these people reads like this:

THINKERS [thing-kers] noun: A cross between strategy-types and suity-types, they ask a lot of questions and listen very carefully for the answers. They're problem solvers, punctual and know how to drive business results. They know how to get shit done.

TINKERS [ting-kers] noun: Creative-types and producery-types who pull things apart and put them back together again. They hit things with hammers and fiddle with knobs and buttons. They experiment and play and build. They know how to get shit done.

You need both types of people for a great agency. The idea of Thinkers and Tinkers extends through the agency, with staff able to choose their favourite example for their business cards. Pictures of famous Thinkers and Tinkers are on the website and displayed on walls in the office. Each is represented as half Thinker and half Tinker, because that's where the magic happens.

The Little Green Book

The final reason to believe we can deliver is our 'Little Green Book', which is a collection of thoughts and approaches from people we admire. We aim to be a hyper-connected agency. We believe full service is dead and that no one agency can do everything, but we know who to call to fill the gaps.

These are the three reasons to believe we can deliver on measured magic and help ensure the agency is structured to provide it. The next part of the puzzle is to define what the brand looks like — the fun bit.

The name game

We wanted our name to relate directly to 'measured magic'. We came up with 'Merlin & Sherlock' as a homage to measure and magic and a dig at those who name their agencies and businesses using their surnames. Here are five reasons you shouldn't name your company after your surname:

1. You sound narcissistic.

2. For people who do not own the company but have aspirations to do so, it makes it harder to have a sense of ownership.

3. It's not in itself a guiding brand — the name can inform the work and the brand — but the brand itself still needs definition.

4. It makes a promise that the founder (or spirit of the founder) will always be in the room (for good and bad).

5. It doesn't feel overly creative.

(There are exceptions to the rule, and you can still be a great business even if your business is named after the founder. In advertising, this includes Droga5, Wieden+Kennedy and Saatchi & Saatchi, all of which are exceptional agencies.)

I still remember Cuz turning his computer in my direction and saying, 'I thought of this'. It read 'Thinkerbell'. I instantly liked it because it screamed measured magic, and it felt like a name we could own. Thinkerbell is also soft and feminine, which felt different from other agency names. However, there is still an issue that everyone automatically says 'Tinkerbell' even when they know it's Thinkerbell. Our neurons are deeply wired. I keep telling myself it's a positive thing—but I'm not so sure.

Logo a go

The logo was easy to develop. Thinkerbell is a clash between thinking and magic, so we integrated Rodin's classic sculpture *The Thinker* with the wings of Disney's Tinker Bell (see figure 7.3).

Figure 7.3: Thinkerbell logo

I love the logo. Someone told me they thought it looked like a dance party raver sitting on a rock after a huge night out feeling a bit ashamed of themselves. I love it nonetheless. The ability to succinctly summarise the brand in a logo is essential because many communications possibilities exist in under a square centimetre of real estate: the symbol on an app, an email signature, the profile picture next to a social media handle, or email signature.

How it carries through

The final elements we chose were typeface, colours (pink, green and charcoal), beliefs and values, all of which help to guide the agency.

We also use the words 'measured magic' throughout the agency. The week begins with the 'Measured Monday' staff meeting where we talk through the upcoming workload for the week. The week finishes with 'Magic Hour' where magic sometimes happens. The other manifestation of measured magic is the work we produce for clients.

When new employees begin at the agency, we give them a book that captures these principles, so they know about the agency brand. What we've done well, and what I'm most proud of, is how tightly we've defined our brand. A smaller company (ours has 40 to 50 people) is easier to brand than a larger one, but the principles still apply. In our second year we were voted Adnews Creative Agency of the Year and Mumbrella's Emerging Agency of the Year — so it's working well so far.

Many marketers don't adhere to one of the fundamentals of marketing: the brand comes first. At Thinkerbell, we apply the formula BXB4CX — brand experience before the consumer experience. This formula is relevant because of the current excitement around CX.

Positioning guides everything the agency does. We think it allows us to enjoy a little patch of real estate in our clients' and potential clients' minds that makes it easier for them to choose us rather than another agency. The importance of positioning isn't shared by everyone. Let me tell you about the biggest cage fight that's ever happened in Australian marketing circles. Okay, it's the only fight — but it's been pretty exciting.

The Great Brand Positioning Rumble

There are two alpha-male marketing science gorillas battling it out for the attention of marketers. Both Mark Ritson and Byron Sharp are welcome voices in an industry that for many years promoted BS and puffery. I know both chaps, and their opposing views are matched by their opposing personalities. Sharp is a neat, pedantic, self-confident and often dismissive academic. Ritson is a free-wheeling, expletive-laden street-fighting Yorkshireman. (Actually, I'm not sure if he's from Yorkshire, but if he isn't, he should be.) Both are brilliant and both have made significant contributions to marketing and marketing science. These two heavyweights are in intense disagreement about one thing: brand positioning. The argument is more interesting because 'brand positioning' is a marketing fundamental — arguably THE marketing fundamental. By calling it into question, they are challenging one of the central tenets of marketing: that a brand holds a place in a consumer's mind and purchasing is based on this positioning. There's no doubt that brand positioning is out of style and under attack. The skills required to conduct brand positioning are on the wane in an industry drowning in data. Brand positioning is the place the brand holds in the consumer's mind. It is a set of associations and impressions that are carefully constructed and controlled. If your brand captures and holds these associations, then consumers understand the promise you offer and think of you when the need for the category is triggered.

Byron Sharp is critical of brands that spend too much effort on brand positioning, especially if they're trying to be differentiated. He says a brand should focus on its distinctiveness. Ritson holds an orthodox view and believes positioning is one of the foundations of marketing. In 2018, Ritson offered this advice in *Marketing Week*:

> ... *Working out the attributes you want to stand for, which ones you want to grow, which you want to reduce and whether — a year from now — you have achieved your ends, are among the most worthwhile and valuable activities a marketer can ever commit to.*[32]

After persistent online debate, I understand the two have since made up.

Byron Sharp was a keynote speaker at a conference I run called Marketing Sciences Ideas Xchange (MSIX). Before the conference we met over dinner, and I asked him about the value of brand positioning. He said to look at the key players in any significant category. Banking, for example. What sets one major Australian bank apart from another? The answer is nothing. They don't have separate positioning because brand positioning is a waste of time. He said it's fine to workshop the values of your brand and what it stands for, but suggests you don't spend too much time doing this.

I don't know if Sharp's views on positioning have been widely adopted and if agencies are consciously not worrying about the positioning of brands. In my experience, marketers are worried that their brands are under-developed and poorly thought through. When a company hasn't crafted its brand, and when the positioning isn't clear, it makes every other decision difficult. I'm a big believer in brand positioning.

The practical attack on brand positioning

Is the fact that brand positioning doesn't happen with as much care as it used to because people don't have the time? And if they don't have the time, is it because of the increasing complexity of their jobs? Marketers have moved from responsibility for around five channels to hundreds. Their tasks are increasingly complex and the demands on their time infinite, making it hard to ensure the basics are covered.

An interesting data point on brand positioning is figure 7.4. When I asked marketers the one thing they'd like to spend more time on, just over 20 per cent said brand positioning. Three times as many said understanding the consumer. The lack of clarity around understanding the brand affects my daily consultancy and agency work. Brands with a coherent and agreed-upon brand positioning are diminishing, but required more than ever. Without it, how can you be sure everyone is working towards the same North Star or organising thought?

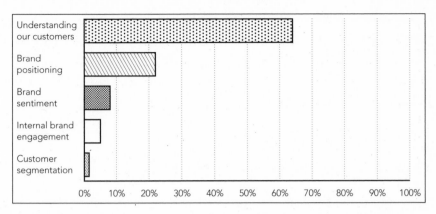

Figure 7.4: desired time and resource allocations of marketers

At Thinkerbell, we pride ourselves on ensuring we understand, define and disseminate the brand, no matter the challenge. Here's a case study that reveals how we do this.

Defining Vegemite

At the end of 2018, Thinkerbell won the account for the iconic brand Vegemite, which had been with the same advertising agency, JWT, for over 70 years. When Australian company Bega Cheese Ltd took control of Vegemite from Mondelez, the advertising account was put to a tender. After an initial meet and greet 'chemistry' session, Thinkerbell was asked to pitch along with four other agencies. The briefing document asked for one thing: iconic communications befitting an iconic brand. Thinkerbell asked for Vegemite's existing brand positioning and was met with the surprising news that there wasn't one, at least not in recent corporate history. We knew we needed to create brand positioning and capture this in a brand book to ensure everyone who worked on the brand knew what it stood for.

The pitch request was this:

To develop and articulate a new distinctive Vegemite Brand communication platform which integrates and delivers on our three strategic imperatives to win the hearts and minds of consumers, to grow the brand in 2018 and beyond.

Here's roughly the process.

1. Understand the vision of the business

What ultimately does the business want this brand to achieve?

This was contained in the brief — for Vegemite to find its voice as an Australian icon. For years, people knew this but Vegemite didn't act in this way and the communications didn't reflect its iconic status.

2. Define the market or category

What are the key dynamics of the category we want to embrace?

Again, this work was already done. Vegemite was in the 'spreads' category, meaning the share of market would come from other spreads, including honey, jam and so on. The challenge was that Vegemite's share of the market had dropped, along with household penetration. We also knew the number one driver of choice in the category was 'taste'. That is, the client wanted us to talk about the taste of Vegemite as iconic in Australia.

3. Develop the central brand idea

I'm not sure how other people do this, but I always jump to the answer and flesh out the central thought from there. The brief was tight: find a way to talk about taste that would also position Vegemite as an iconic brand. The target audience was pretty much every Australian, so we didn't need to spend time building a customer profile or delve into the current audience. We decided to look at pre-existing research. What made Vegemite so iconic? What was its history? Why was a weird-tasting spread so popular? We wanted to avoid the trap of only talking about taste and creating marketing that was similar to that of other spreads in the market. But how could we ensure that the brand had taste cues while referencing its iconic status?

We needed to discover the relationship between taste and Australia. To help with this process, we tracked down food scientist Dr Sigfredo Fuentes. Originally from Chile, Sigfredo is now based at Melbourne University in the School of Agriculture and Food. Thinkerbell team member Andre Pinheiro interviewed Sigfredo at his stark university office. Following the chat, Andre rang me from the taxi and, paraphrasing Sigfredo's responses, said, 'Taste is a cultural construction. Australia created the taste of Vegemite. Vegemite tastes like Australia.' We didn't know at the time that these words answered the question of why Australians love Vegemite. It implied Vegemite is for everyone, which fits neatly with country's sense of egalitarianism. We used the line 'Tastes Like Australia' to suggest everything about the nation is encapsulated in a little jar. Your definition of Australia is how Vegemite tastes.

4. Flesh out the brand

The next step is to flesh out the positioning and capture it in a brand book, which we created for Vegemite. Although mostly symbolic (the pitching agency couldn't know the brand as well as the business), it's a discipline that we are keen to encourage. The brand book represents, in my mind, one of the fundamentals in a marketer's bag of tricks. When the entire organisation and brand ecosystem (client, staff, agency and trade partners) understands the brand book, it's easier for everyone to communicate the brand consistently and coherently.

The brand book

The brand book is a way of capturing information to organise and communicate the brand (with the caveat that 'everything communicates', from packaging to pricing to advertising, CX and UX; it's all communications). I summarise information within the brand book as the brand positioning.

Brand positioning has a chequered history and different meanings depending on who you ask (see: the brawl between Mark Ritson and Byron Sharp). The discipline of marketing has been terrible at its nomenclature and, ironically, the branding. Philip Kotler defined brand positioning as 'the act of designing the company's offering and image to occupy a distinctive place in the mind of the target market.' But these days, positioning seems to be playing second fiddle to other execution elements. Consequently, I think it's worth defining what you mean by brand positioning and how you use these elements to organise what the brand is about and how to communicate it. The process can be accomplished within a week or three and doesn't depend on consumer insight, although we are happy to incorporate it if needed.

The best way to capture information for a brand book is in a way that matches the brand. It doesn't have to be a book, for a start. A book is just a practical way to start. This is what I like to cover in a brand book:

◆ *The backstory.* What has the brand done before, and why does it exist? This can be freshly created for a new brand. Existing brands can capture the best-of history. With new brands, if I understand the motivation for the brand, it helps me know the orientation of the brand and its aspirations.

◆ *The consumer.* Who does the brand appeal to and why will they choose to buy this brand? As is often the case, the consumer for a particular category can be everyone — if that's the case, state it. But perhaps give a reason why people prefer your brand over others in the category.

◆ *The proposition.* This is the central reason the brand exists. If possible, express it as a rallying cry to be used internally and externally. Can it be captured in one phrase? Thinkerbell's is 'measured magic'. Another term for this is the central organising idea.

◆ *Reasons to believe.* These are the statements that support your central organising idea. How can you back it up so it's not just bullshit? At Thinkerbell, we support our central organising idea of 'measured magic' with our 4 Leaf Clover, Thinkers and Tinkers and Little Green Book. Each demonstrates reasons to believe we can deliver on the promise of 'measured magic'.

◆ *The benefits.* This is the way your brand is meant to make people feel emotionally, and the benefit of your brand rationally.

◆ *The values and personality.* There's been much debate around brand imagery and its association with brand preference. It's fair to say that identifying a few words that sum up your values and personality is helpful, no matter what the science says. At the very least, it helps to maintain consistent communications and guide internal staff on how the brand should behave.

◆ *The distinctive assets.* How does the brand express itself? In what way is the brand famous or could be famous? This is important and acts as a shortcut and signifier for the brand. They help to build distinctiveness. Think of Coca-Cola's red colour, contoured bottle, ribbon and sans serif font. We applied this to Vegemite, from the font, jar, colours, diamond shape, old song and a new song. Thinkerbell's distinctive assets include the little Thinkerbell man, the 'Thinker and Tinker' naming convention and the combination of pink and green colours. To build assets over time, they need to be consistent. Fame and ownership are critical requirements for substantial, distinctive assets. They need to be recognised by others and be strongly associated with your brand.

◆ *The actions.* How does this brand behave? This is perhaps the hardest element to summarise in a brand book but one of the most pertinent. Many marketers spend way too much time wondering what the brand stands for, rather than how it will behave in the world. Crack that, stick to it and you'll spend a lot less time wondering if ideas are right.

◆ *The strategic pillars.* What are the top three to five achievements for the business over the next three to five years? This incorporates high-level communications strategy rather than brand positioning, but it helps in understanding a brand.

5. Develop the communications

Once the overall platform, idea and position were developed for Vegemite, the communications was relatively easy. We suggested three to four ideas that all fit within the central organisational idea: 'Tastes Like Australia'. The client chose the weirdest and most wonderful of them all. The idea emerged from trying to determine the 'ingredients' for Vegemite. There's the obvious material — Skippy, Bondi Beach, Aussie Rules football, the Barrier Reef, Rebel Wilson epitomising Australian humour, BBQs. The more controversial choices included Pauline Hanson saying 'Please explain', convicted criminal Chopper Read, and John Howard attempting to bowl at a cricket match for military personnel in Pakistan. The idea also came to life in outdoor advertising and social communications.

Testing lunacy

How do you know it's the right idea? There's a subsection of marketing research called advertising pre-testing. It asks a consumer how they think they'll react to a new advertisement. There's next to no evidence to support its efficacy. I think it's lunacy. To this day, advertising pre-testing generally involves market research respondents viewing a cartoon version of the ad and being asked if they think the cartoon ad would make them buy the brand in the future. It drives me nuts.

An alternative to pre-testing is seeking the response of subject matter experts through structured interviews. Although it's uncharted territory, we used this approach for the Vegemite advertisement. Each marketing expert received a rough cut of the ad in a variety of contexts, including a line on its own, outdoor advertising, digital and video advertising and promotional ideas. A structured questionnaire accompanied the assets to capture their thoughts on the various pieces of communication.

Here's how several people viewed the same piece of communications. Let me introduce Mark Earles, who has held senior positions in some of the world's largest and most influential communications companies. Dr Peter Field has worked on planning and consultancy at iconic agencies such as Abbott Mead Vickers BBDO, DDB and Bates and Grey. He's also written *Marketing in the Era of Accountability*, *The Long and the Short of It*, *Brand Immortality* and *The Link Between Creativity and Effectiveness*. Faris Yakob is an old mate, an award-winning strategist, creative director, public speaker, geek and author of a great book called *Paid Attention*.

While all four loved the tagline 'Tastes Like Australia', and their overall response was positive, they were cautious about referencing

Pauline Hanson and posed great questions. Earles warned the campaign to 'avoid simple nostalgia' because it risks easy dismissal. Field thought it was 'infinitely flexible and has legs — I could see the idea playing out in fresh ways over many years'. Little did he know just how well it would play out in his home country of Britain during the 2019 Ashes, which you'll read about shortly. I took note of his advice about the budget. As Field put it, 'To some extent, the outdoor requires scale and domination to achieve the iconic effect you mock-up'. Faris said, 'Love it, mate. I love catchy songs and jingles and that the yellow is strong and awesome. It's fun. Tastes like Australia is gold and no-one else could do it.'

This feedback gave us the confidence to include the image of Pauline Hanson in the advertising, although it did cause a stir.

Now that everyone knows the brand...

Here's a real-world example that demonstrates the advantage of a tightly aligned brand. Our agency, Thinkerbell, picked a fight with Marmite during the 2019 Ashes series. After reading an article in Britain's *Daily Mirror* headlined 'Free Marmite being handed out at the Ashes to prove it's better than Vegemite', I sent this email to the marketing manager of Vegemite, Matt Gray:

Sent: *Wednesday, 7 August 2019 8:13 AM*

Subject: *It's our national duty to respond*

https://www.google.com.au/amp/s/www.mirror.co.uk/money/free-marmite-being-handed-out-18845123.amp

Here are some possible responses

1. *A full-page ad in the Mirror in the UK saying*

    ♦ *It's been brought to our attention that Marmite have been handing out free jars of Marmite to prove it tastes better than our Vegemite — well please, Marmite, save your money. To the English palate of course it does.*

- *You see, Vegemite is a far stronger taste, made of resilience and fortitude with a dash of cunning and guile. Vegemite tastes like back-to-back 100s on your return test. Because Vegemite Tastes Like Australia.*

There could be other options Jim / Cuz / anyone. But this is pretty funny. We could then direct tweet all the players and ask them to retweet this. Thoughts??

Adam Ferrier — Founder / Consumer Psychologist

THINKERBELL

Seven minutes later, at 8.20 am, was a reply from Marketing Manager Matt Gray, who, along with his internal stakeholders, was completely aligned on the brand, so could act quickly and from the gut.

This is bloody brilliant! Love it, let's do it!

This led to a flurry of activity.

From: *Adam Ferrier*

Sent: *Wednesday, 7 August 2019 9:10 AM*

Subject: *Re: It's our national duty to respond*

Guys

Jim is turning my ramblings into a proper ad.

Margie and I have put calls into buying a full-page ad.

We'll develop a social strategy reaching out to the players to see if they'll retweet it, etc.

Nikia this is the bit where I have no idea what I'm doing. Could you help wrangle the idea?

Matt, the cost of a full-page ad in the Mirror will be the only sticking point. But it's also the fun bit. Kind of needed as the foundation.

Adam

Less than 24 hours later, this full-page ad appeared in the UK's *Daily Mirror* (see figure 7.5). Forty-eight hours later, Marmite responded with a reference to Australia's ball tampering incident from 18 months earlier.

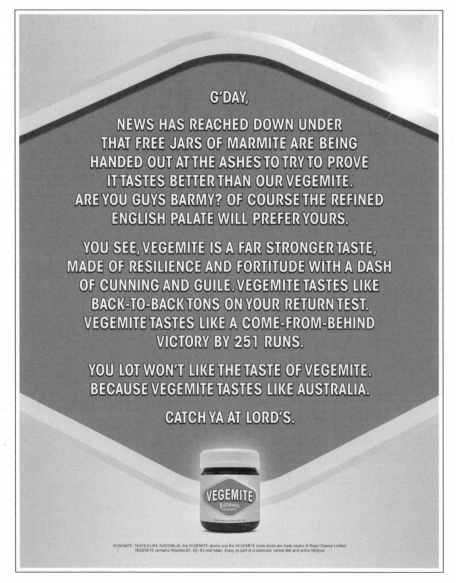

Figure 7.5: *Daily Mirror* **Vegemite ad**

Vegemite's next move (see figure 7.6) was to place another newspaper ad on day one of the second test at Lord's Cricket Ground. It referenced the fact that the colours of the Marylebone Cricket Club are the same as Vegemite's: red and yellow. It cheekily suggested that members wearing the red and yellow striped suits and ties were indicating their support for Vegemite. We also offered to swap their jar of Marmite for a new jar of stronger, bolder Vegemite.

By day three of the Test, Marmite's creative team upped the ante by handing out sandpaper swatches to the crowd, again referencing one of Australia's darkest days in sport, the shocking ball tampering incident.

Our team changed tack, and created an advertising jingle for radio. As Britons applied Marmite to their toast that morning, they heard this song on English radio:

We feed our team Vegemite to help make 'em strong and mighty, to battle through the cold and rain of a summer in Ol' Blighty,

We'll need our strength and energy to continue to impress, despite some shonky catches and a dodgy DRS.

The Poms have brought back bodyline to force our early exit, but our boys will still be standing long after Boris decides on Brexit.

If we start each day with Vegemite the Ashes are a shoo-in, regardless of their carry-on, their jeering and their booing.

It gives us the resilience to get back up off the deck, even after copping a bouncer to the neck.

Love or hate your Marmite, England, Aussies are decided, we all adore our Vegemite, it keeps us all united.

With Vegemite on our side there'll be no Ashes failure, because victory is sweet and it tastes like Australia.

Figure 7.6: Vegemite's response to Marmite's response

It was accompanied by a press release quoting Matt:

> *We are increasingly disturbed by Marmite's insistence they won't be tampering with their Marmite. If people love or hate it then surely they can do what we've done and find a taste that unites the country. We don't want to mention Brexit or a parliament divided, but we think they are a manifestation of a country disjointed.*

The initial full-page ad in the sports section of the *Daily Mirror* cost $29 000, reached 40 million people, and generated around $6 million worth of PR for Vegemite. Thinkerbell was able to act quickly because we were clear about the brand and what it stands for. Many organisations can't act in such a decisive manner because they don't understand the messaging of the brands they work for. As you can see in the example of Vegemite, decision-making was swift and streamlined.

It starts with the brand

Subsequently, after the Vegemite work we've had lots of discussions around if it 'insight driven' or not. All I know for sure is that there were not a whole lot of Vegemite customers waiting for us to pick a fight with Marmite. It was a bit of fun, born from a great mutual understanding of the brand, what it stands for, and its objectives.

chapter 8
gonzo marketing 1: fire the CEO

Brands pride themselves on 'integrated marketing communications', which means all communications are linked. Marry this with the idea that 'everything communicates', absolutely everything, and the entire business should ideally be oriented around the same brand idea. The central brand idea should become the North Star and drive the look, feel and meaning of everything. This includes the website design, the swing tag, the UX and CX, the advertising and even the branding on salespeople's cars. Brands are at their best when everyone in the organisation is aligned around a single idea. This is known as 'inside out' marketing.

Gonzo marketing

For me, the most useful articulation of inside out marketing is from the first marketing book I read. The book was called *Gonzo Marketing: Winning through worst practices* by Christopher Locke and was recommended to me by a friend in advertising. No-one I know has ever read it, but it's the inspiration for this and the next chapter.

Gonzo marketing is adapted from the ethos of gonzo journalism, the most famous proponent of which was Hunter S. Thompson. Thompson's book *Fear and Loathing in Las Vegas* is held up as the quintessence of the genre. Gonzo journalism collapses boundaries between the reader, the content and the author. There's no claim of objectivity because the author is part of the story. As Wikipedia describes, 'It is an energetic first-person participatory writing style in which the author is a protagonist, and it draws its power from a combination of social critique and self-satire.' In gonzo marketing, there is no 'us' — the marketer — and 'them' — the consumer. The two are merged. This chapter discusses how to do gonzo marketing, from the inside out, starting with the board.

Corporate governance and me

I'm excited about this heading. Several years ago I didn't know what 'corporate governance' meant and until recently I would have dismissed it as boring and irrelevant to brand understanding. I now understand the imperative of corporate governance to brand understanding at the heart and the head of the business. (This is a tortured way to describe the board and the CEO.) If gonzo marketing is a clever way of employing inside out marketing, then the most 'inside' part of an organisation is the board. The board and its governance structure set the framework for the entire company. If a board understands the power of a brand and how to build one, then the company has a good chance of being successful. How many boards understand something as difficult to pin down as 'brand', emotional connections and creativity?

A 2019 joint study by *The Financial Times* and the Institute of Practitioners in Advertising found that over half of business leaders rate their knowledge of brand building as average to very poor. This is despite 83 per cent of business leaders in the study believing that brands continually deliver the bottom line. Brand building is important, yet many business leaders just don't get it. The title of the report was 'The Board–Brand Rift: How Business Leaders Have Stopped Building Brands', and it paints a negative picture of corporations and their capacity for strong brand intelligence. That is, the ability to understand and prioritise the brand. It was based on a self-reporting questionnaire sent to business leaders who were readers of *The Financial Times* across the world. It found the lack of knowledge was most apparent when comparing channels that are thought to be most effective at building brands. Over half the leaders thought social media was one of the most effective channels for brand building. The report claims it's just about the worst for building brands.

The issue isn't just for large organisations with an established board structure. I see the same issue with startup brands and Silicon Valley culture in general. Here, technology reigns supreme along with the skills of the coder and developer. But what's their North Star? What's galvanising different work streams and agile stand-up meetings? To say it's 'the brand' is almost heresy. However, it's what everyone is trying to create. Without the brand, I don't get what the North Star for these companies could be, which may be why many of them don't succeed.

For years, there was prevailing wisdom that to be influential, the chief marketing officer (CMO) needed to understand the language of the boardroom. Now the opposite is more likely to be the case. Today, boards across the world are hiring prominent marketing people to help them incorporate the magic of marketing. Richard Branson and Indra Nooyi understand marketing. Before they died, Steve Jobs, the co-founder of Apple, and Ingvar Kamprad, the founder of IKEA, understood marketing. They understood the importance of brand. Their boards recognised and prioritised brand-led thinking. Until recently, boards didn't know where the real power lay — it's with the people who understand this intangible value.

Today, boards ranging from established publicly listed companies to startups are creating businesses built around brands. They understand that the brand is central. Marketing is not advertising. Marketing is the brand, and the brand is everything. Some of the more engaging conversations I've had are with those who want a board that marries good corporate governance with creativity and innovation. I applaud moves to inject more creative thinking at a board level because if it doesn't happen at the very heart of the organisation, it's less likely to occur in the rest of the company.

The Bon Jovi of the board room

One of the more eccentric people I've met in my time is the enigmatic Finbar O'Hanlon. Finbar is a self-proclaimed doppelganger for an ageing Bon Jovi. He's always decked out in leather, with big teased peroxided hair and metal on every finger. As a musician, Finbar toured the world and recorded with bands such as Limp Bizkit. He's also an innovator and inventor, especially in the areas of video and music. He created the personalised video technology platform Linius Technologies, which is a publicly listed company. He seamlessly sways between business, music and ideas, although his physical expression screams ROCK! Finbar is an experienced board director, and nothing gets him more fired up than a conversation about board corporate governance and its relationship to creativity. He now helps other companies as a board consultant and coach, and he cuts a distinctive figure in corporate Australia.

I asked Finbar how a company or business should structure its board to reflect the brand. In other words, how do you create a board that embraces inside out marketing? He said he starts by modifying the board's core founding documents. Board architecture is important to him, along with expert category-based sub-committees (Innovation/ Disruption/ M&A, Legal, HR, Finance, Compliance etc.). Finbar said,

Although this sounds like common sense, skills based matrixes to award board positions are still not as common as one may think. Further for those that do, marketing/brand/innovation/ creativity are rarely discussed at board level, let alone do they have representation.

I then asked Finbar about the board obsession with managing risk, and how to manage creativity within that context. Finbar believes a board needs to reduce risk but also hold creativity and marketing in the same regard as legal, finance and governance.

A part of this would be making sure decision making is evaluated on understanding the risk effects of not making a decision and valuing the effects of not understanding the value of marketing and of true innovation in the risk matrix. Make sure the board

understands 360-degree risk and the components that run into it. For example, without understanding the top 5 companies that may disrupt you in the next six months, you are not managing risk (innovation subcommittee, M&A). Also, without understanding the changing customer desires, you are not managing risk (advertising and marketing subcommittee). Very rarely is a board involved in the brand. Often boards do not even understand the brand.

Finbar doesn't ask brand and creative people to better understand the board, but instead demands that the board understand the brand. If there's an appreciation of the importance of brand at the board level — with no us versus them — it's easier for the entire organisation to be brand focused. This is branding from the inside out, or gonzo marketing.

Inside out with superannuation

One of my clients is a small but rapidly growing superannuation company. Superannuation helps policyholders build a nest egg for a financially secure retirement. But the industry has had a rocky time of it of late with the Financial Services Royal Commission uncovering some dubious business practices. With this as a backdrop, they had asked us to help with their brand positioning because they wanted a strong and consistent story for their staff, customers and business stakeholders. The project started with a series of interviews with the key people in the business to ascertain their points of difference. Many spoke of their diligence and careful approach to business. This was solidified when we interviewed the chairman of the board, what he said really helped us understand the company and what set it apart.

When the chair started to educate me about superannuation, I admit my eyes began to glaze over. He told me that in Australia, there are two types of superannuation funds. Retail funds are beholden to shareholders and short-term profits, and industry funds are often beholden to unions and vested interests. However, this fund's board has a skills-based matrix for appointments (with brand and media representation), no vested interests and a governance structure that enshrines this requirement. The chair believed their point of difference was its governance and board structure.

With these insights, my agency created a proposition that reflected their sensible and considered place in the market, and their approach to growth. We wanted to capture the advantages of the board structure in the brand positioning because if we got this right, then it would be easier for everyone in the company to understand the brand. We wanted simple, easy to understand language that reflected a fair and diligent approach to corporate governance and superannuation. After creative development and refinement, we developed a platform idea and brand line that has words to the effect of 'Reassuringly Dull'. I love this because the proposition emerged from the business's governance structure. It was a truth about the brand. I cannot share with you the fund, nor the final positioning developed — it's just a little early. However, suffice to say it's diligent, careful and risk-averse nature ensures a fair, reasonable, and relatively predictable return to members — and that's a good thing.

The principles of 'reassuringly dull' permeate through the company, including its internal communications. The investment team loves it because it communicates their sensible investment decisions. The human resources team loves it because it captures the spirit of the organisation. And the marketing team loves it because they can stretch and play with the truth of the proposition. The idea has power because it came directly from the governance structure of the board, and the vision of the chair when he established the board.

Do we need a marketing department?

An investor friend of mine has this rule: never invest in an organisation with a marketing department. He believes a separate marketing department stops those in the rest of the company from taking responsibility for marketing. Everyone, no matter their position, has a role to play in building the company. I think it's an interesting and provocative stance designed not to remove marketing, but ensure everyone in the organisation appreciates that the entire business is marketing. Everything communicates and everything helps to build the overall brand experience.

Unfortunately, if you took a bunch of marketers from the 1990s and asked them to set up a marketing department today, they'd probably do the same thing. It would feature a marketing department hierarchy and areas of specialisation further down the chain. This style of marketing is predicated on other people building, making and managing what we do with the marketing team taking it to market.

I believe this is how many people in startups and technology perceive marketing's role. I've watched tech companies create their product with the view that marketing is something that happens in a separate department. I've read several briefs that suggest 'we've built this great thing, it looks amazing, and now we need people to buy it, so we'd better do some marketing'. If you have enough money, this can work. As Robert Stephens said, 'Advertising is the tax you pay for being unremarkable'. If you create an unpopular product, you pay a higher tax. There is an alternative, and that's to include the marketing department in the product's development and ensure it's effectively communicated across every part of the business.

In chapter 4, I mention the Forrester report that argued CX was contributing to the homogenisation of brands. Its advice is to relabel CX as a creative experience. The report suggests:

A key characteristic of this new moniker is the broadening of the channels and executions associated with it. Where customer experience is predominantly associated with owned digital channels, creative experience includes all conceivable brand touchpoints: advertising, content, experiential, digital products, customer service, and more.

This report is in the right zone to be useful.

The historical role of the Chief Marketing Officer was as a head marketer in an organisation, managing the marketing team. In this model, marketing was advertising and promotion or occasionally broadened into product innovation. It was never a company-wide role.

As companies recognise that marketing needs to encompass everything the organisation does, there's an issue of structure. I advocate that the CMO or, even better, Chief Brand Officer, is retained, with marketers deployed throughout the organisation. Their job is to develop brand-led thinking (BXB4CX) no matter where they are within the business. From procurement to new product development, sales or human resources, it is all brand-led thinking.

Do you need a CEO?

Let's take it up a notch. To achieve what I'm suggesting, you may need to sack the CEO. Within an organisation, the CEO runs the show, and the biggest show in town needs to be the value of the brand. At the moment, the CEO is the person that others report to, including the Chief Financial Officer, Chief Technology Officer, Chief Marketing Officer and so on. However, in a model where everyone in the business reports into the brand, then the CEO has to become the Chief Brand Officer. Think of the top brands in the world: the ones that adhere to a central organising thought that is understood across the entire business, and where the brand is the business. There's Virgin, run by Sir Richard Branson; Apple, co-founded by Steve Jobs; IKEA, founded by Ingvar Kamprad. These companies have one thing in common: all are run by 'marketers': people who understood their brand. I love the photo of Steve Jobs arm-in-arm with Lee Clow, chairman and global director of TBWA Worldwide. Clow was responsible for Apple's 'Think Different' campaign used from 1997–2002.

It's beautiful because it shows that even though Steve Jobs had other work priorities, the brand and its communication were second to none. Lee and Steve famously caught up once a week to talk about the brand, its current position and how to improve it. I don't know if many other CEOs do this.

Trade secrets

I don't want to get in trouble for the revelations in these next paragraphs. My lawyer has checked them out and assures me it's good to go, but I'm still a little nervous. (In addition to being an excellent way to get your attention, this is the truth.) Here's what happened. I speak at numerous conferences in Australia and around the world. Usually, at the end of the talk, someone will be interested in some aspect of my presentation and want to chat further. A few years ago, I spoke at a human resources conference and talked about content from my first book, *The Advertising Effect: How to change behaviour* (obnoxious plug). After the talk, a woman approached me saying, 'Adam, I really enjoyed your presentation, and I'd like you to come to Canberra for a chat'. I said, 'Sure, where do you work?' She said I'd find out if I came to Canberra. I was intrigued.

And so a colleague and I flew to Canberra for the meeting. When we arrived at the designated address, we entered an elevator and met a man. The man asked us to leave our bags, watches and phones and to proceed through a metal detector and wait in a room. In the room, my colleague and I had a bit of a giggle and waited. We thought we might be meeting with the Australian Federal Police. Then someone walked into the room and asked us to sign a non-disclosure document. Now that the work is in the public domain, I'm not violating the document. We signed it, handed it over and the person left. After about ten minutes, the woman I'd met at the conference walked in with a few other people and explained that we were at the offices of ASIS. I gave a confident nod. She then asked, 'Do you know what ASIS is?' As my cheeks turned red, I admitted that I didn't.

ASIS is the Australian Secret Intelligence Service. It is Australia's spy network primarily concerned with gathering information of national importance from overseas. ASIS was keen for a rebrand. As you can imagine, this was a lot of information to take in as we sat in a funny little room in a strange big building with three people we'd only just met and whose names we didn't yet know. And so began a relationship that would take many twists and turns over the next few years.

Because it's a secret intelligence service, ASIS was having difficulty recruiting new spies. The recruitment process at the time was generally a tap on the shoulder and an invitation to a meeting. But the agency was keen to diversify its staff. As part of the rebrand, a colleague and I interviewed nearly every intelligence officer that was stationed in Australia, along with the director-general and the second-in-commands. I can still remember the director-general telling me I was the person least like himself that he'd ever met. I love that comment — he was a lovely chap.

Because ASIS is a relatively small organisation, our presence alone shifted the culture and expectations of the agency. Once the central brand proposition was developed, most were on board with the new direction of the agency. I won't disclose what the organisation believed about itself, only that it dialled up its competitive advantage in the marketplace of espionage. The interviews were exceptionally good fun to do.

After the new ASIS brand was embraced internally, we set about developing a recruitment campaign (going from inside out, as gonzo marketing should). We wanted the campaign to be as intelligent as the organisation and allow ASIS to stand apart from ASIO, which many confuse it with. The goal was to reveal the typical experience of an intelligence officer without giving away any trade secrets or compromising anyone's safety. We devised 'The Most Interesting Job Interview'.

I left the agency responsible for the campaign before it was released, but it was executed beautifully. It came to life as an online experience taking people through a mock interview that was both very interesting and very hard. It gave prospective recruits a top-line assessment before inviting them to apply for ASIS. Potential recruits were guided through a five-minute interview exercise in which they completed tasks that approximated the skills ASIS is looking for. It was a prominent and outward-facing brand refresh for ASIS and included a refreshed website and social media presence.

The campaign was a massive success, with ASIS receiving 12 months' worth of applications in only two weeks. The applicants were more diverse and tapped into a new pool of people. This new recruitment campaign also meant ASIS was talked about extensively in the media in a positive way. It shifted momentum within the organisation and was one of the most rewarding and interesting projects I've ever worked on. This type of work doesn't emerge from a marketing department but is reflective of the entire brand working from the inside out.

Think gonzo

The term 'gonzo marketing' may not be well known, but it encapsulates this ideal: an organisation that understands its brand from the top down and the bottom up. When this happens the brand can be actioned at every single touch point. In some cases, a restructure will be needed for brand ownership to exist across the organisation. Others will require more drastic measures, such as appointing a new CEO with brand understanding. Whatever it takes, the brand is everyone's responsibility.

chapter 9
gonzo marketing 2: put the customer second

Sir Richard Branson says one of the keys to his success is a steadfast focus on staff before customers. Branson told *Inc.* President and Editor-in-Chief Eric Schurenberg:

> *It should go without saying, if the person who works at your company is 100 per cent proud of the brand and you give them the tools to do a good job and they are treated well, they're going to be happy.*

When Branson is on a Virgin flight, he wanders around the cabin and chats to the staff to find out what's happening. As Branson sees it, the formula is simple: happy employees equal happy customers. Conversely, an unhappy employee can ruin the brand experience for not only one but many customers. Branson says that Virgin prioritises employees first, customers second and shareholders third.[33]

'The customer is always right' goes the 'how to do good business' gospel. The issue is it's wrong. Yet, companies are told every day to put the customer ahead of the employee. It's a tough situation. If customers believe they're always right no matter how ridiculous their demands, it can make things worse. Customers might bully staff and make it difficult for them to defend themselves. This behaviour also happens online and on social media, where companies can be held to ransom by disgruntled customers who believe they are in the right. Companies must trust their employees and value their resourcefulness when dealing with dissatisfied customers. Inside out marketing ensures the employee is prioritised first. In chapter 8, I discuss the structure of inside out marketing. In this chapter, I'll tell you how to make it happen. Once this is sorted out, you can build demand by focusing on the consumer.

Your employees are media

It's important that each employee understands the brand and feels prioritised. There are three significant trends happening within business that mean every employee is an important stakeholder:

♦   the competitive advantage of service

♦   the all-pervading influence of social networks

♦   the fragmentation of today's workforce.

Service

The technology, artificial intelligence and machine-learning boom means more goods are being produced by machines. But we're also witnessing the rise of the 'experience economy', in which the service around items we buy, rather than just the item itself, is attracting a greater share of value. For example, say a flat white coffee costs $3.50. If that coffee is made by a cool barista in a hip artisan café and delivered by a waiter reciting poetry, I'm likely to pay more because of that experience.

But because humans can be unpredictable, brand understanding is important. The brand becomes the North Star for training and development to ensure everyone is aligned behind the values of the company. This is what we do at Thinkerbell. Another proven way to keep staff happy (and productive) is a creative, inspiring and innovative workplace. These ingredients mean the organisation can get the most from the people who work there.

Social media networks

Social media networks have turned corporate culture from a black box to a glass box. The existence of employee review site Glassdoor and professional networking site LinkedIn means the corporation you work for is on show 24/7. Everyone who works there, or has worked there, becomes a window into that corporation or brand. Their thoughts and feelings about the brand are vital for the business.

Omnipresent social networks mean every employee is an influencer. Whether your business has five or 5000 employees, each is more invested in your company's success than those who don't work for the brand. It's crucial they are armed with the right messages and, better yet, the best ways to promote the company. Before social media entered our lives, it was popular to quote Robin Dunbar, the Oxford University anthropologist and psychologist who claimed the average human had around 150 friends in their social network. Now, it's impossible to estimate the number of people your organisation can influence. Let's just say it's a lot.

Fragmented workforce

The increasingly fragmented workforce means people enter and exit your business with greater frequency. Casualisation means the barriers to entry are lower, but tenure is less likely. Job sharing, contracting and outsourcing are on the rise as businesses create greater flexibility in the workplace. In some organisations, it's exploitative. I think this is the case with Uber. Regardless of your views on this, it's a fact that more people enter and leave your workplace than ever before. It means more people touch and feel your brand and become more invested in its success.

What's the first day like for new employees? What is their induction into the brand and business? What tools are they given to understand it? How do they commit to building the brand? What language does your organisation employ? What are the new skills people need to learn about your way of doing things? How do they get to know your brand, invest in it and live it?

These three elements reinforce the importance for organisations in ensuring employees don't merely understand the brand. They need to understand they *are* the brand and play an important role in its dissemination.

Embrace internal engagement

When I work on projects involving an organisation's employees, I receive an 'internal engagement' brief. Internal engagement used to be viewed as the poor cousin to consumer engagement and limited to the distribution of stress balls, screensavers and ringbound pamphlets. As part of this book, I surveyed high-level marketers and CEOs on their priorities within their organisation. Figure 9.1 was particularly interesting. Everyone said 'meeting the needs of the customer and understanding their needs' was most important, ahead of brand and communications strategy. The least important priority was internal brand engagement. Sir Richard Branson didn't complete the survey, but I wonder what his response would have been.

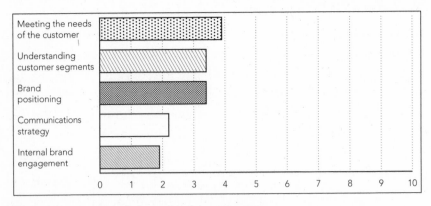

Figure 9.1: ranking of marketing priorities

But there are some green shoots. Internal engagement is on steroids in many large technology-driven companies. There is the budget for it, and they also treat their brands like an ecosystem inviting staff, suppliers and customers to trade shows and festival-type conferences. Accounting software company Xero and customer management software company Salesforce are examples that come to mind. Taking their lead from cult-like companies such as the Steve Bulmer–led Microsoft, these tech-driven companies are spending more time, money and resources on making sure their staff understand what the brand and company is about.

Tackling the faceless ride-share companies

In the age of Uber, would you want to be in charge of marketing for the taxi industry? Liz Attia became head of marketing at the taxi company 13cabs at a time of intense disruption in the sector. Her task was to transform 13cabs from a service into a brand. Taxis had to stand for more than ferrying passengers from A to B. For decades, the taxi industry had no significant competitors because government regulation made it difficult for others to enter the market. It meant the existing taxi service was coasting. Before Uber and other ride-sharing operators hit the market, the passenger experience in a cab was unpredictable. You didn't know if the car would be clean or the driver would be rude or would even turn up. Passengers didn't believe the company's tagline, '13cabs will get you there'. When ride-sharing services hit the market, passengers had greater choice. It also meant drivers had options other than working for 13cabs.

I clearly remember the first meeting with Andrew Skelton, CEO of Cabcharge, because it was important for both parties. Cabcharge was evolving from dispatch and logistical services with an affiliated taxi fleet of 8500 to consolidate operations under a single national 13cabs brand and 13cabs app. It was under pressure to select the right agency to help it with this period of transition, and Thinkerbell was in its infancy. Andrew listened as we presented our credentials and our assessment of

13cabs. We said the service was patchy and that some of the drivers were rude, unprofessional or disengaged. But we thought an ethnically diverse driver base was a positive because it offered the chance for passengers to chat with someone from a different background.

Andrew then told us his story. When he was in high school and at university he worked in taxis to help pay his way, and he quickly became a manager at a local taxi organisation. After finishing university, Andrew practised as a lawyer in mergers and acquisitions. But taxis, he told us, were in his blood. He was passionate not only about taxis but their role in society. According to Andrew, becoming a taxi driver was often the first job for an immigrant and important in helping them to integrate into their new country. He was disappointed and ashamed that ethnically diverse drivers were seen as a weakness in the company. The taxi industry has done more for inclusion than just about any other industry.

After winning the account, we started by drilling down with management about their customers and the 13cabs brand. Uber was the main competition. But at the time, Uber was facing negative press around the world for a series of internal and business-related issues. Uber, according to the narrative, would do anything to increase its revenue, including controlling drivers through micro rewards and positive reinforcement to keep them driving for longer. But it was still hard for them to make decent money. Further, Uber gave the appearance of not caring about the disruption it was causing to communities of taxi drivers. Uber's image was of a faceless corporate giant interested in profits over people. Well, it wasn't completely faceless; its then CEO, Travis Kalanick, contributed to the perception issues following a series of well-documented indiscretions that ultimately caused him to resign.

Uber offered an extremely efficient service, mainly through its app. 13cabs matched this with their app. However, 13cabs had an advantage: its full-time drivers had greater allegiance to the company than those from Uber. Further, 13cabs had strong connections in the suburbs they served. Pubs, clubs and RSLs relied on cabs, as did hospitals and other care organisations. These taxis transported hospital patients, war veterans and the elderly—none of whom ordered a cab from a smartphone or paid using a credit card.

From these insights, we developed a central brand proposition: 'people moving people'. People are on both sides of the equation—passengers and drivers. We established the features and benefits of the brand, its value and personality. A brand book captured the proposition.

The way in which we communicated the brand was vital. We put the drivers first and the customers second. We knew we needed to improve the fleet and improve perceptions. A full internal engagement program is now underway. We did three things when launching the new brand:

1. Cars were re-badged to appear modern, cleaner and fresher.

2. All communications featured staff from 13cabs going about their day to amplify the 13cabs proposition of 'people moving people'. We developed a strategy revealing the benefits of a people-focused culture for customers. The advertising put a spotlight on the inner workings of 13cabs. Radio ads featured real phone calls to the call centre. TV and cinema ads highlighted people across the company, including Nick in lost property, Karen the contact centre supervisor and taxi driver Saeed, who's been driving for 27 years. Each spoke about 13cabs and its service. Further, in digital media, we did something kind of clever. We identified when and where ride-share companies had surge pricing and ran ads that said, 'With 13cabs, there's no surge pricing, just Serge driving'. (Quite a few of the drivers are named Serge, which is handy.)

3. In partnership with the Nine Network, we created a 12-part TV show called *Anna Gare's Cab Fare*, which made a strength of what was previously perceived as a weakness—the ethnicity of cab drivers.

In the series, celebrity chef Anna Gare rides in 12 taxis around Australia, chatting to the driver, asking where they are from and what food they like to eat. Anna then agrees to meet the driver at their home with their family and re-create their favourite dish. The show worked as a substantial piece of internal engagement because we communicated in a positive fashion. We asked drivers to be part of the series and received hundreds of applications before deciding on the final 12. When the show aired, the driver was featured in local media and showcased in internal communications. 13cabs continues to hero the driver in a series of initiatives that highlight an ethnically diverse driver base that's proud to work with the company.

These initiatives allowed 13cabs to remain competitive despite massive pressure and media spend by the ride-sharing companies. Over two years there have been some noteworthy results. Over 2 million people have downloaded the 13cabs app. Ninety-nine per cent of drivers have rebranded their cars to read 13cabs, and negative sentiment on social media has reduced almost entirely. Further, Cabcharge's share price increased 30 per cent,[2] and the company has the confidence to expand and grow, with several exciting initiatives in the pipeline. The team at Thinkerbell is enjoying the challenge.

The campaign so far was achieved without conducting consumer research. Now, however, we're adding tracking capability and market segmentation. We're also gathering upfront insights to find out what else people want from 13cabs. But the company knows what is most important to it and the shining light. And that's 'people moving people'.

Finally, it's the smallest of tweaks, but the line has changed from '13cabs will get you there' to '13cabs, we'll get you there'. It's a reminder that people are the most critical part of the business.

The tech startup and branding from the inside out

Many technology startups have founders who are developers, or who come from the technical side of the business. The company reaches a certain size, receives funding and then it's decided it needs to do marketing. Marketing for these companies is often 'acquisition', and generally doesn't sit at the centre of the business. There are some obvious exceptions where marketing feels indistinguishable from the product, but this is rare.

TRIBE is an influencer marketing platform company where the brand permeates the entire business. I've sat on its board and invested in the business. It always strikes me that everyone who works there gets what the business is about. Everyone understands its tone, personality and vision of the brand. Everyone is on the journey.

I remember an early all-staff meeting at TRIBE when it had approximately 20 employees. (There's now over 80 across four countries.) Founder Jules Lund gave an impassioned speech explaining the company was in its startup phase but growing quickly. He said that one day, the company will be sold or cease to exist. Those gathered could be on the journey for as long as they liked. From inception to startup to scale up to exit, you can learn and have fun doing this job. I loved the honesty of this talk. It was the first time I'd heard a business owner speak so openly to staff about one day selling the business, but framing it as a positive.

It should be no surprise that TRIBE is one of those brands in the market that has a cult-like following with Jules and his disciple, Ant, running the show. I asked Jules how he keeps his people so enthused and aligned with the brand.

Adam: How do you understand what's on and off brand for TRIBE?

Jules: A brand is simply a personality. The easiest way to ensure it's cohesive across all touchpoints is to have it filter through one lens. I felt the same with the social accounts for my radio shows. It really should be one voice. Otherwise it's simply a split personality, which is unnerving. I love branding…I just love building a personality from scratch. After a while, once your team has become familiar with it, and you've documented it as well as you can, it can scale beyond one guardian.

Adam: How do you ensure everyone in the organisation understands this?

Jules: As often as possible, expose your team to the spirit of your brand, especially internally. Tell the story over and over and over. There shouldn't be an external and internal look and feel. It's one brand you all belong to. Then empower them with the assets and guidance to express your brand in that unique dialect. And if anyone steps outside of that, punish them. Punish them good. Joke! Sort of.

Adam: And do your staff promote TRIBE?

Jules: Have a look online. Our people are our greatest ambassadors. They are constantly talking us up, and constantly talking about TRIBE. We share a lot, and I guess it's a really sociable company so yeah they promote us.

Customers are Number 2

To recap, get employees to rally around and understand the brand first. The great businesses and business leaders from around the world subscribe to this philosophy. For too long, internal engagement was viewed as the poor cousin to consumer-facing advertising. As brands increasingly move into the service space and people become more instrumental to the delivery of any branded good, employee engagement around the brand becomes paramount. It's no coincidence that the most recent Australian company to be valued at over a billion dollars is called Culture Amp, a business that allows other businesses to measure workplace engagement.

chapter 10
embracing the negative

If you work in marketing and brand building, here's a warning. There's some challenging material ahead. I want you to come to the dark side and embrace the negative. I realise most people avoid facing the negative aspects of life. They don't want to be depressed or to observe sad, bad or mad things in the world. Life is hard enough as it is and there's rarely a yearning for more negativity. It doesn't mean you shouldn't go there. In fact, embrace the dark side and you'll be a lot happier.

The yin yang symbol is not just a cool tattoo

The yin yang symbol is a tattoo classic, especially if you grew up in the nuevo hippie, 'no logo' era: the 1990s. If you haven't seen it, it's a circle with an S down the middle with black on one half of the circle and white on the other half. A white dot and black dot sit within their colour opposite, mirroring each other along the middle of the circle. My ex-girlfriend had one and thanks to her, I discovered its meaning. She told me, very earnestly, that it reminded her to find balance in life. Even though we broke up, we're still friends and she now happily lives at a small hippie commune in the hinterland.

The yin yang symbol encapsulates the idea that two oppositional forces can come together to form a complementary whole. There's light and dark, night and day, fire and water, masculine and feminine. When you look at a tree, you can see its trunk, resplendent branches and leaves, but beneath the ground is the root system that mirrors what you see above the ground. When you shine a light on an object, it creates a shadow. The shadow is a function of the object. You can apply yin and yang thinking to brands. The oppositional force for toothpaste is cavities. The oppositional force of coffee is lethargy.

Yin and yang are based on Chinese philosophy and became popular long before the 1990s tattoos. It dates from the third century BCE with Chinese cosmologist Zou Yan describing several interchanging stages of life. Yin is moody, feminine, black and dark. In nature, it is north, water (transformation), cold, valleys, old, earth and winter. In numerology, it's even numbers. In life, it's passive. Yang is masculine, white and light. In nature, it's south, fire (creativity), sun and heaven, mountains, warm and young. In numerology, it's odd numbers. In life, it's active. Nothing is purely yin or yang. I can hear you saying, 'Adam, that's all very interesting, but show me how it applies to brands'. Your wish is my command.

Dirt is creativity

For years, the branding for laundry detergent Persil/Omo was based on an aspiration to be clean, white and bright. The tagline over decades was 'Omo adds whiteness to brightness' with pre-2000s advertising showing frustrated and annoyed homemakers attempting to remove dirt and stains from the family's washing. That is, until they use Omo. But the company was losing market share to P&G's laundry detergent, Tide.

In 2006, the 'Dirt is good' campaign was born. Rather than point to Omo's ability to remove stains, the product embraced its yin — dirt — rather than just its yang — whiteness and brightness. This change of approach liberated millions of kids because their parents were able to think to themselves, 'It's okay if little Alex plays in the dirt'. Former global brand director for Unilever's laundry business David Arkwright developed the insight that children learn life skills while playing and getting dirty. He said they found '... a deep connection available, via the deep insight that "If you are not free to get dirty, you cannot experience life and grow".[35]

The depiction of a mother trying to suppress her feelings of frustration about the inevitable occurrence of dirt was abandoned. If 'white' was order, control and work, then 'dirt' was freedom, creativity and play. These were aspirational qualities for a parent to embrace. The more dirt there is, the happier you are. As Arkwright explains, 'Now, the narrative is that dirt equates to creativity; and parents aspire to have creative, free-thinking and playing kids, as opposed to those locked into pristine-clean conformity.'

Advertisers don't tend to reference yin and yang when developing ideas, but many consider oppositional views when developing a campaign. I think yin and yang may have informed some of the thinking behind the 'Dirt is good' campaign. The yin and yang symbol can act as a potent reminder that what you avoid should be what you embrace.

Wabi-sabi is not just a sushi restaurant

For many years I've ordered a wonderful tuna salad from a great little Japanese restaurant called Wabi-sabi. I've always liked the name. The Japanese have a reputation for perfection. Think of beautifully wrapped apples from the market, immaculately raked sand gardens and elegant ceramic bowls. Think of the ability to miniaturise, replicate and copy everything perfectly. But this reputation is misleading. Japanese aesthetics and beauty often employ the concept of wabi-sabi. If you look more closely at a raked sand garden, you'll see it's far from perfect. There are always a few misplaced rocks in the garden that the rake has worked its way around, creating a near-perfect feel. Beautiful high-end Japanese ceramics are never perfect and often a little off-kilter or wonky. 'Wonky' is such an inelegant word to describe something so lovely. Wabi-sabi is the beauty of the imperfect, impermanent and incomplete. It is a beauty of things modest, humble and unconventional.

Like yin and yang, wabi-sabi encapsulates one thought. 'Wabi' is a kind of perfect beauty caused by just the right kind of imperfection, such as asymmetry in a ceramic bowl. A 'perfect' but soulless machine-made bowl would, according to wabi, be less aesthetically pleasing. 'Sabi' is the kind of beauty that can only come with age — possibly a problematic concept in our youth-obsessed culture. In marketing and advertising, rather than the term wabi-sabi, we use the words authentic and real.

This wasn't the case in the latter half of the twentieth century. Historically, marketing was modelled on mass production and mass distribution and supported by mass communications. Back in the 1950s, 1960s and 1970s, perfectly made goods were an indication of quality. As times and trends changed, perfect replication has gone out of style. Thanks to demands for ethical supply chains and a desire for unique items that stand apart from the crowd, mass production is facing challenges. Consumers want one-off, locally made or non-processed products. Flaws signify that an item isn't mass-produced. 'Authentic and real' says this brand or product was created especially for you and has not been mass-produced. It's been made with love and care.

And, paradoxically, imperfections in brands and products substantiate this story. Many handmade clothes have a label that reads 'Please note imperfections or irregularities in the colour of this garment are because it's handmade'. This confirms the garment is a one-off rather than mass-produced.

I encourage marketers to practise wabi-sabi.

Leonard Cohen's 'Anthem'

In 2008 I was fortunate to see late musician Leonard Cohen perform under the stars at a winery. We had front row tickets and sat on a blanket with a bottle of wine, making it a rather unforgettable night. Everything was perfect. Even the support act was my all-time favourite musician,

Paul Kelly. The reason Cohen was touring was that his manager had ripped him off and he was broke, an irony not lost on me: I was able to enjoy his brilliance because of his misfortune.

Cohen's music explores life's darker themes, perhaps best exemplified in his beautiful song 'Anthem'. I think the lyrics, talking about how cracks and imperfections are what let the light in, reveal an exquisite understanding of wabi-sabi.

Obviously Cohen isn't the only artist to tap into the power of embracing the dark side of human existence. The fact that we can enjoy the feelings of being sad, lonely, angry or depressed while listening to music or enjoying art in general has always been the gift of artists, but for a long time ignored by marketers. Where the arts have been happy to delve into the dark side of the soul to help people express their unexpressed feelings, marketing has all but tipped its toe into this dark pool of emotion.

As an industry, marketing doesn't like cracks. It prefers the glib, the superficial and the perfect. A consequence of this approach is a lack of authenticity, which is why Cohen's lyrics are so powerful. In order to create strong marketing, I suggest abandoning the need for perfection.

We all cast a shadow

Carl Jung was a student of the world's most famous psychologist, Sigmund Freud. Jung is best known for his theories on the shadow, or unconscious, aspect of our personality. He believed this unexpressed and repressed part of our personality drives most of our behaviours. The shadow is the part of the personality the conscious ego does not identify, even if we go into therapy. It's easier to remain ignorant of your shadow than confront it. However, not facing or accepting your shadow can have significant consequences. As Jung wrote, 'Everyone carries a shadow, and the less it is embodied in the individual's conscious life, the blacker and denser it is'.

According to Jung, the goal is to assimilate the shadow into our being. The term he used was 'individuation'. Without individuation, two aspects of the self are not integrated, and the individual is not as powerful as he or she could be. 'Acknowledgement of the shadow must be a continuous process throughout one's life.'[37] I think marketers can open a range of new opportunities by assimilating the shadow in their campaigns. Let me explain through the example of Batman, which is a representation of this concept.

Batman

During my final year of university, I lived off-campus with two other would-be psychologists in a suburb called Reedy Creek (which we renamed Rudy Crack—we were university students, after all). My flatmates were Shay and Simon. Shay was my ex-girlfriend, which made flatmate life difficult, but that's a story for a different time. Simon is still a very close friend. He's softly spoken and quietly enigmatic, with a passion for Carl Jung and session musicians—those who play with famous bands but rarely have their names in lights.

When we were at university, Simon made sure that we came home by 4.30 pm to watch the cartoon series of *Batman*. Each weekday, the three of us would watch the show as a bit of an in-joke. But Simon became annoyed when we talked about the absurdity of twenty-something psychology students rushing home to watch a kid's cartoon every afternoon. During one episode, crime boss and enemy of Batman Rupert Thorne says: 'The brighter the picture, the darker the negative.' I asked Simon to explain the quote.

In that episode when Rupert Thorne remarks 'the brighter the picture, the darker the negative', he essentially was recapitulating one of the pillars of Jung's contribution to psychology. Namely, there is an inverse relationship between the polarities of our various selves. Jung asserted that if we persist in shining a light and focus exclusively on only one side of these polarities, it creates an imbalance that can sometimes manifest into difficult protracted patterns in our lives.

Given that, it appears ironic that it was a crime boss who provided this pearl of wisdom and not Batman. What that suggests is that the shadow lurks deep within everyone, not just the villains. So that begs the question: what kind of greatness lies deep within the Joker underneath that maniacal face of make-up and chaos? Furthermore, if this theory of the shadow holds true, what remains repressed in Batman's shadow underneath all of that armour and heroic pursuits?

It seems that both are operating from a trauma, subsequently relying exclusively on the 'brightness of the picture' as a way of coping and getting on with their lives. But this continues to bring them imbalance. What if both Batman and the Joker were to therapeutically work with their shadow energies and explore the true nature of their trauma? What if they were able to truly feel their feelings from long ago? Perhaps there would be no need then for either of them to continue with their social masks and cowls. Simon and I have discussed Batman and other superheroes in much detail over the years. We even made a short film about Batman's motivations called *Chiroptophobia*.

Simon believes that because superheroes are accessible and obvious, they can play a therapeutic role in society. I believe they can also inspire marketing.

Batman marketing

Brands that are brave enough to tap into perceived negative attributes and engage with the dark side can create greater authenticity. Here are examples of well-known brands expressing their dark side and, in so doing, finding strength and authenticity.

- ◆ *Avis.* They're number two. 'We try harder.'

- ◆ *KFC.* When UK stores ran out of chicken, an ad featured a KFC bucket with the letters changed to FCK and 'We're sorry' written underneath.

- ◆ *Volkswagen.* When launching in the United States, the headline read 'Lemon'.

- ◆ *Picnic.* This ugly-looking chocolate bar used the tagline 'Deliciously ugly.'

- ◆ *Norman's Steakhouse.* The ad for this restaurant in Brisbane features the line 'The worst vegetarian restaurant in Brisbane'.

- ◆ *Omo/Persil.* 'Dirt is good'. Put another way, if Omo is Batman, dirt is the Joker.

Brands can sometimes stumble onto embracing the dark side and communicating negatives from time to time. Few brands consider this strategy systematically or strategically.

Negative emotions

As mentioned in chapter 2, Dr Paul Ekman is the world's leading scholar in emotions. He identified micro facial expressions described as 'involuntary emotional leakage', in which lies can't be hidden. Ekman also identified six primary emotions that are observed in cultures across the world, including pre-literate remote tribes: anger, disgust, fear, sadness, surprise and joy.

Primary emotions reside in a part of the brain called the amygdala that sits at the stem of the spinal cord. It's often referred to as the 'reptile brain' because its structure is also found in the brains of reptiles. Over time humans developed a limbic brain that emerged in the first mammals, and a neocortex, which assumed importance in primates. This is where advanced cognitive functioning occurs.

Something is interesting about the first four primary emotions outlined by Ekman. They are negative. 'Surprise' incorporates positive and negative affect. Happiness is the only positive emotion on the list. But it's these emotions that helped us to survive. We avoided drinking mammoth's milk (disgust), we ran away from sabre-toothed tigers (fear), and we attacked anyone that tried to harm our offspring (anger). But this means we are born with a tendency to focus on the negative. When bad news hits the amygdala, it's processed and stored in our long-term memory more efficiently than positive information. Isn't that interesting for marketers and advertisers?

What happens when a species is hardwired to pay attention to the negative but lives in an Instagram culture hell-bent on staying positive and portraying aspirational versions of everything? The same goes for marketing, where gloss and shine still dominate. According to Associate Professor of Psychology Jonathan Adler, we ignore negative emotions at our peril. His 2012 study found that experiencing and embracing both positive and negative emotions was a predictor of improvements in overall wellbeing. He discovered that ignoring or suppressing negative feelings didn't help people feel better.[38]

In the study, 47 adults in psychotherapy were asked to complete questionnaires that measured psychological wellbeing and write a private diary that was rated for emotional content. The study found that people who had both positive and negative emotions during the therapeutic process were more likely to report improvements in wellbeing than those who didn't report negative emotions (or admit they had them). The study concludes: 'Experiencing happiness alongside sadness in psychotherapy may be a harbinger of improvement in psychological well-being.'

I was fascinated by this study because it's a scientific version of Batman's 'the brighter the picture, the darker the negative' concept — and yin and yang, for that matter.

Negative cognitions

In addition to emotions, the brain is also hardwired to process and remember negative thoughts. But it's difficult to untangle emotions and thoughts. Thoughts affect how you feel, which affects how you think. Mental processes are essential in decision making and for evaluating if an experience is positive or negative. We tend to be drawn to, pay attention to and remember bad news, ugly things and mistakes. This has been labelled the 'negativity bias'. Here are some examples of the negativity bias:

♦ In one study, 74 per cent of the words subjects used to describe personality were negative. When thinking of someone, we tend to remember their negative or unattractive features rather than positive ones.[39]

- Two people come to you and demand your attention immediately. One has negative news, while the other has positive news. Which are you more likely to listen to? According to research,[40] it's the negative one.

- Psychologist John Cacioppo examined participants' brain activity as they looked at three types of pictures: positive, negative and neutral. Brain activity was significantly higher (meaning it processed more information) when participants looked at negative imagery.[41]

In 2013, Canadian researchers from McGill University tested whether it was readers or journalists driving negative political news content.[42] In their study, participants were told they were part of an experiment to track their eye movements as they watched TV news stories. To allow the software to adjust to their eye movements, they were asked to read newspaper articles about Canadian politics. They could choose which articles to read and the pace at which they read. But there was no eye-checking technology. The researchers were interested in the nature and type of articles chosen by the participants. In this experiment, most wanted to read negative stories even though they said they preferred to read positive news stories.

A similar logic applies to positive or negative headlines as revealed by the web advertising platform Outbrain. In a study of 65 000 titles, Outbrain compared positive superlative headlines (e.g. 'Best', 'Always', 'Greatest'), negative superlative headlines and no superlative headlines. The study found that headlines with positive superlatives performed 29 per cent worse, and headlines with negatives performed 30 per cent better. The average click-through rate on headlines with negative superlatives was 63 per cent higher than positive headlines.[43]

We are attracted to negative headlines. But when you ask newspaper readers if they want more positive stories, they answer 'of course'. This study shows they don't. As an advertiser, if you can find negative content about your competition, people will listen to it. Politicians know this strategy very well: it's why scare campaigns exist. The reason they resonate with voters is because of negativity bias. Advertising that aggressively undermines its competitors stands out. If you're a challenger brand, one option is to pick a fight. If you're a declining market leader, it could be time to highlight the weaknesses of your number two.

Why are marketers reluctant to be negative if it works? In short, it's probably related to that thing we call 'the brand'. During election campaigns, politicians can ditch long-term thinking and replace it with a win-at-all-cost mentality. They can be negative without worrying too much about the long-term impact on their brand. Marketers, on the other hand, have a brand to build and protect. They are not just interested in short-term attention and sales but on building the brand over time. Studies reveal well-liked brands are likely to be purchased more often. It's hard to like someone or something that is constantly negative.

The alternative to perfect

In 1966, psychologist Elliot Aronson studied people's perceived levels of competency and attractiveness and the impact of failures and mistakes. In his study, known as the 'pratfall effect', subjects listened to a recording of someone auditioning for a game show and answering tough questions. When the questions came to an end, the game show hopeful makes a mistake, such as spilling a cup of coffee. This was the 'pratfall'. Others answered tough questions but weren't as clumsy. And here's an interesting result. Those who correctly responded to questions and spilled the cup of coffee were ranked as more likable and respected than those who answered the questions competently but didn't spill anything. The blunder made the subjects more likable. But, and it's a big but, the effect was only evident for those in the competent group. For those in the incompetent group who did poorly on the game show questions, the effect didn't kick in and had the opposite effect. You can only be clumsy if you're already competent. Messing up draws people closer to you and makes you more human, while perfection creates distance and an unattractive air of invincibility. Don't be afraid to step into the dark from time to time.

Embrace your weakness

We developed the concept for *Anna Gare's Cab Fare* for 13cabs (discussed in chapter 9) with Tim Fletcher, an independent TV producer. I loved the idea of embracing a perceived weakness of 13cabs (the ethnic diversity of its drivers) and turning it into a strength. Even in the world of internal change management, it's a strong concept. The idea of focusing on weaknesses rather than strengths was partially inspired by the coaching philosophy of Australian tennis legend John Newcombe, AO.

For those unfamiliar with him, he was a larrikin tennis player who achieved world number one ranking in both singles and doubles tennis in 1970 and 1971. He was famous for his handlebar moustache, which was reportedly insured for $13 million. Newcombe also captained the Australian Davis Cup team in its heyday. When he retired from playing, he became one of the world's most successful tennis coaches with a practical and straightforward approach to assessing a person's tennis game.

When assessing a player, John went through the facets of the game, including forehand, backhand, serve, volley smashes, court speed, endurance, and so on. He then ranked each of these disciplines out of 10. Imagine a player received rankings as shown in table 10.1.

Table 10.1: assessing a player

Facet of game	Score
Forehand	8
Backhand	3
Serve	9
Volley	6
Smashes	8
Court speed	3
Endurance	8

Guess which facet John would focus on improving? Most start with strengths, but not John. He began by focusing on weaknesses. In this example, he'd begin by working on the backhand and court speed because this is where the most significant improvements can be made. If the player's serve is rated 9 out of 10, it's bloody good, and focusing effort to shift it from a 9 to a 10 isn't worth it. Perfection is paralysis. How can you improve a slow player with a weak backhand? Put the training focus on the weakness. The backhand may never be world-class, and the court speed will never be a strength, but significant gains can be made in both areas.

I asked Newcombe about his beliefs and attitude toward coaching. When I asked about focusing on strengths versus weaknesses, he said, 'If someone does not want to embrace working on their weakness, then you are wasting your time working with them.' It's the same for coaches. Newcombe told me:

> *Tennis is a game requiring many different strokes. A good coach should recognise he will not have the best answer on every one of these strokes for every pupil. I believe I have the answer for 90 per cent but for the 10 per cent I am not sure, I would seek out the best person I knew. Many coaches are reluctant to do that.*

In understanding and embracing weaknesses, there's significantly more room for growth according to one of the legends of world tennis. The same could be said for leaders of a company — and the more vulnerable, the better. Well, sort of. For 13cabs, driver engagement would have received a very low score on the John Newcombe tennis assessment, and that's why we started by fixing this first.

Why the Fonz was cool

Back in 2003, I did a Clinical Psychology thesis titled 'Identifying the underlying constructs of cool people'. I knew it would have commercial application because unlocking the elements of cool is, for some, marketing's holy grail. For others, it's just a lame dinner party conversation, but that's okay. Anyway, I discovered a lot about cool and recently repeated the research to find out if it stood the test of time. It does.

One of the first things I discovered about cool was its cultural context. According to historian Dick Pountain, the term 'cool' was associated with the persecuted, downtrodden and disempowered. It has its origins with slaves that were put in chains and transported from Africa to America.

Everything was taken from them: possessions, loved ones and freedom. The one thing that couldn't be taken was their soul.

Cool stemmed from the 'cool poise', the look of deadened affect projected by those in chains when brutalised by their 'masters'. The cool poise, later referred to as a mask of detached emotional irony, projected this meaning: even though you've taken everything from me, you can't touch my soul.

Cool has been associated with the beatniks, the hipsters (the first time around) the punks and the rappers. Cool was a descriptor for those who never quite fitted in. This changed with the commercial appropriation of cool. Cool has been captured and fed back to us in an aspirational loop that means cool people are now at the top of the tree. These are the ones we all aspire to be. It hasn't always been this way.

The person who best exemplifies cool to me is the Fonz from 1970s sitcom *Happy Days*, which depicted American life in the 1950s. The Fonz was the cool guy with his leather jacket, blue jeans and nonchalance. So how was cool portrayed? Firstly, the Fonz had a mask of detached emotional irony. He perfected the cool poise, often accompanied with a laconic 'eeyyyyyy'. Secondly, he rented a room above the Cunninghams' garage. The Cunninghams were a squeaky-clean, cheesy and wholesome-as-apple-pie family. They were not cool at all. The Fonz didn't know his parents and was a bit of a drifter. He was an outsider who stood outside the mores of society. He didn't go to university or college but was a mechanic. At the same time, he was moral, intelligent and, on many occasions, the oracle of empathy and wisdom for the rest of the gang. The cool guy was nice and empathic.

My thesis identified five factors that make someone cool:

1. self-belief and confidence

2. understated achievement

3. defying convention

4. caring for others

5. connectivity.

The Fonz exemplified point 4, caring for others. Cool was left-leaning, humanitarian and inclusive. Cool politicians were always left-wing rather than right-wing (think Bill Clinton, not George W. Bush). If you want to take the cool test I've included it in the appendix. I've included it because when I talk about it, people often ask me if they're cool. With this simple test, you can find out. (If you are cool, then please use your powers wisely.)

Cool people know what it's like to not fit in. The idea of not fitting in can be useful for organisations and brands, especially those that want to cultivate an 'us versus them' mentality. I'm familiar with the sentiment of 'We don't fit the mould, so we have to create our own thing'. It's the ethos at my agencies Naked Communications and Thinkerbell. Here's where this gets interesting. It turns out not fitting in makes you a good manager.

Why rejects make good leaders

As Steve Jobs said, 'It's more fun to be a pirate than to join the navy'. From Jesus Christ to Robin Hood to Sir Richard Branson, history is filled with outcasts who not only assemble followers but effectively lead and manage those followers. Whether from fiction or reality, it creates a strong narrative and galvanises people to fight injustice and be part of an 'us versus them' mentality. There's research that proves outcasts can make good leaders. And for every weirdo who feels like they don't fit in, this should offer some hope.

Elaine Cheung and Wendi Gardner published a paper titled 'The way I make you feel: Social exclusion enhances the ability to manage others' emotions'.[44] They argue that throughout history, those rejected or shunned by their peers can develop an advanced level of empathy and understanding that allows them to become better managers of others. Published in the *Journal of Experimental Social Psychology*, the research suggests the desperate need to reconnect can encourage people to develop or enhance the emotionally intelligent skill of empathy. In so doing, people like you more because you understand them. Being rejected by others, it would seem, is an excellent way to develop leadership skills and likability. I'll summarise two of their studies.

In one experiment, around 100 participants were asked to write one of two stories. Group A wrote a story about a time when they felt they did not belong. Group B was asked to write about the layout of their local grocery store. After this exercise, all participants were asked to write some strategies they'd use if they had to cheer up a friend or calm down an angry friend. Those who recalled a time in their lives when they did not belong came up with more ways to make their friends happier or calmer.

In another study, around 70 people were broken up into pairs. One subject in each pair would play the role of someone looking for a job, while the other would play the role of a job coach mentoring and advising the job candidate. The coaches were assigned one of two writing tasks. One group of coaches wrote about a time they experienced social exclusion, and the other group wrote about a time they felt socially accepted. The coaches would then advise the job applicants. The applicants with a coach made to think about a time they were socially excluded rated their coaching as significantly better than the other group. They left their sessions feeling more inspired and liked their coaches more. The socially excluded coaches were more effective at managing the emotions of their job applicant subjects. The researchers conclude, 'These findings suggest that social exclusion may enhance the ability to manage others' emotions and that this enhanced ability may evoke greater liking from others.' I often joke with friends that if I could change one thing about my time at school, it would be learning to conform and fit in with the others. But this research demonstrates just how powerful and useful not fitting in can be.

Men's mental health is about admitting you may not be healthy

Man Up was a three-part documentary series and social awareness campaign presented by Gus Worland, funded by The Movember Foundation, with insights from Professor Jane Pirkis, the director at the Centre for Mental Health at the University of Melbourne. The project investigated why Australia has such a staggeringly high suicide rate for men (it's the most common way for Australian men aged 15 to 44 to die[45]) and what could be done about it. After the TV series aired, an advertisement was broadcast on TV and across social media with the goal of increasing awareness of the issue. This is how we created it.

The first insight for the campaign's development came from lauded co-creator of the advertisement, Adam Hunt. Adam observed that *we rarely see men cry on TV*. Part of the *Man Up* series was about encouraging men to express their emotions. Showing men crying on TV could have a 'social-norming' effect, encouraging men to feel more comfortable, or feel it is more acceptable, to express themselves emotionally.

The next insight came from digging around the self-help section of a bookshop and realising that *young boys are just as expressive as young girls*. Each of us is born with an ability to express ourselves when we are sad, deprived, uncomfortable or angry. We cry. But somewhere along the way, men are taught to not cry.

The final psychological insight was a psychoanalytic concept that has stayed with me for years — *depression and anger are two sides of the same coin, or sadness is anger turned inward*. If boys are unable to express their feelings, those feelings can be bottled up or converted to anger.

These three insights were circulated and bounced around until we arrived at the idea of showing images of men at different ages crying. However, as they grow older, they cry less and instead, become more angry. The voice-over challenges men to express themselves when feeling down. The ad can be found by searching 'Man Up campaign' on YouTube. It's had over 50 million views — all organic — that's a lot.

At its heart, the campaign promoted the message that it's okay to be vulnerable. It's a campaign I'm really proud of.

Celebrate flaws

This chapter implores individuals and businesses to not be so hard on themselves. Even better, embrace, celebrate and amplify your weaknesses. Your weaknesses are where your character lies, and can also endear you to others. Brands, businesses and people spend too much time trying to hide their flaws when they should be celebrated.

chapter 11
creating weakness

In the many focus groups I've been involved in, not once has a participant said, 'I want the shopping experience to be more difficult, and I want the product to be more complicated to use'. I'm pretty sure no-one at an IKEA focus group said, 'Make it harder for me'. As outlined in chapter 5, IKEA places several barriers in a consumer's path, but it remains one of the most successful companies in the world. Paradoxically, the irritating shopping experience and need to construct the furniture yourself mean consumers value the brand more highly. This chapter builds on the ideas outlined in chapter 10 and offers practical ways to make brands more sticky in the mind of consumers through creating weakness. You can:

1. force friction

2. be wasteful

3. make mistakes

4. make a mess.

This chapter builds on the ideas outlined in chapter 10 (so if you are skipping chapters, read the last one before you read this one) and offers practical ways to make brands more sticky in the mind of consumers by creating weakness.

1. Force friction

'What's different here?'

As we glide through the day, most of us operate on autopilot (or System 1 thinking, as discussed in chapter 3). This is especially the case with people glued to their phones. So how do you make people pay attention if they're about to encounter something dangerous, such as a railway line? New Zealand rail company KiwiRail faces this issue every day. In New Zealand there are several urban level crossings, which means pedestrians walk across rail lines. Reports from train drivers and CCTV footage revealed many pedestrians weren't paying attention and were placing themselves at risk. Some pedestrians crossed as the alarms still rang, walking after one train had passed but without knowing if another train was coming in the opposite direction. Many people wore headphones or had their faces buried in their phones. KiwiRail needed to find a way to get people to pay attention when they approached the railway.

During Rail Safety Week in 2016, the Conscious Crossing experiment took place. KiwiRail and advertising agency Clemenger BBDO used the insight that the more familiar you are with an environment, the harder it is to get your attention. It decided to create a continually changing environment by installing movable rail fences on either side of the rail line. But the fence configuration was frequently changed. Sometimes there was a zigzag path, other times it was an S shape. Each day pedestrians were forced to take a different route through the crossing. It's very clever.[46]

Forcing people to think is often more desirable than making it easy for them not to think.

What will it take to make you stop?

If you ask drivers who've been on the road for some time to 'Please stop and take a break', some will, but many will not. NRMA Insurance asked for advice for a campaign to run during Easter 2019. What would it take to convince drivers to pull into a 'Driver Reviver' site and recharge before returning to the road? I'm sure you've driven past many on long-distance trips. NRMA Insurance wanted drivers to interrupt their desire to continue driving, pull over and have a break.

1. We commissioned market research agency YouGov Galaxy to find out why people don't stop at Driver Reviver sites. Four in five Australians admit they ignore advice to stop every two hours, saying they want to arrive at their destination as soon as possible. We hoped this research would shine a light on the issue.

2. NRMA Insurance created outdoor advertising with the line 'What will it take to make you stop?' Each included unexpected, attention-getting lines such as the one shown in figure 11.1.

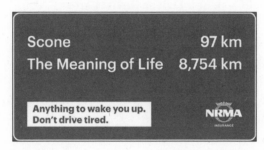

Figure 11.1: NRMA sign

3. Selected Driver Reviver sites had kooky offerings to lure drivers to pull over and take a break. They included:

   ◆ the chance to play ping pong with tennis legend Pat Cash (see figure 11.2, overleaf)

   ◆ people dressed as giant kangaroos handing out chocolate

   ◆ Elvis impersonators singing by the side of the road

   ◆ edible insects offered to drivers.

Figure 11.2: Pat Cash at a Driver Reviver site

This encouraged people to break from their System 1 mindset long enough to judge if they should continue driving or take a break. And the good news is many did take a break. The number of cars that visited the sites increased by 73 per cent. The campaign was covered in the media 162 times, including the evening news.

Someone is watching you

Water conservation is an ongoing issue in Australia, particularly with climate change. During the Millennium Drought, water levels in Melbourne dams reached an all-time low, and the Victorian government introduced the 'Target 155' program. This encouraged residents to restrict their water consumption to 155 litres per person per day. Suggestions included using a four-minute egg timer while showering, collecting cold water in a bucket before the water becomes hot, and to turn the tap off while brushing your teeth. The campaign was successful, with many individuals and businesses changing their behaviour. And, most importantly, water usage dropped. Many households even replaced their grass lawn with artificial lawn.

In 2018, Melbourne's largest water provider, Yarra Valley Water, asked my agency for advice on how to get people to conserve water. But there was no explicit hook to hang a campaign on. There was no new legislation restricting water use. And there was an added difficulty that, because most water use happens in the home, it's harder to influence behaviour. We looked at previous campaigns. Successful programs were generally associated with water-saving reminders inside the house, such as egg timers or blue digital shower timers. According to research,[47] such devices are more successful than broadcast advertising in changing behaviour. So this was an excellent place to start.

Research company Nature confirmed the bulk of water usage now happens inside rather than outside the home. The 'tut tut' look of a neighbour as you furtively water the lawn on a non-watering day is absent inside the home. How could we create an object that wouldn't be ignored, and that watches how much water you use? Marketing sciences suggests those most likely to 'listen' to the objects are children. But we had to devise a system that would appeal to everyone in the household. It had to be like *The Simpsons* and speak to all ages and stages. Psychologists have studied so-called 'watching eyes' and found people are more compliant and law-abiding if they think someone is watching them.[48]

Using these insights, we created 'The Water Watchers'. These are a range of tiny silicon figures that are placed in the shower and near other taps in the home to remind people to use less water. It's currently being trialled in Melbourne.

I'm writing about it here because it's a great example of creating forced friction and breaking habits. The little Water Watchers will act as a roadblock to people's habitual and unthinking use of water. Much like the NRMA Insurance example, and the Conscious Crossing, it forces them to think about and reconsider their behaviour.

2. Be wasteful

In advertising, it's the waste that has an impact.[49] This means the communications we deem to be waste because we can't attribute where a message lands may connect with infrequent buyers. The authors of a study on this, also discussed in chapter 3, make the same point about high production values in advertising. If an ad appears to be expensive, it's more likely to be trusted because it's from a business that has committed to spending resources. The foyers in bank buildings in the Victorian era were richly decorated with marble and panelled wood. Consumers felt they could trust the bank because it had resources to burn on frivolous things like a beautiful foyer. (Recall the examples in chapter 3 of the peacocks and fat older men who drive Ferraris to imply abundant resources to waste on silly things.)

Convince consumers your message is important by being wasteful. I always think of those working in public health when I talk about this principle. Have you had an appointment with a physiotherapist who gives you a photocopied piece of paper with exercises you need to do? Do you ever do those exercises? What if they were photocopied on quality paper or in a fancy book? You might take the instruction to exercise more seriously. The notes themselves, and not just the content, would feel important and worth following up.

A perfect marketing example is naming rights for sports stadiums. When Aussie Home Loans started making waves in the home loan market, it asserted itself as a credible player by acquiring naming rights for the Sydney Football Stadium. From 2002 to 2007, the stadium was named Aussie Stadium. The message implied they were a market player because they were big enough and profitable enough to name a stadium. Sunk costs demonstrate confidence and commitment, and if it attracts attention, consumers often follow.

Another example of waste being effective is search engines retrieving results for the user. Professor Michael Norton has studied the importance of installing counters so people can observe how many options the algorithm is working through before finding the perfect match.[50] A visual representation of what the search engine is doing, rather than instantly finding the best option, increases user satisfaction.

3. Make mistakes

Earlier I mentioned the 'pratfall effect' in which people who make small mistakes are perceived as more likable. Think of someone who accidentally spills a cup of coffee. If they are otherwise competent, this mistake makes them more likable. It turns out the 'pratfall effect' applies to people and brands, and to robots as well. A 2017 study by the University of Salzburg found people prefer to interact with imperfect rather than perfect robots. They could relate to a robot that makes a mistake and learns from the mistake, in a similar way to human learning. The robot's mistakes were identified but it was still rated as more likable than the robot that performed the task perfectly. It's believed robot designers are now incorporating flaws into robot design. Researcher Nicole Mirnig said, '... instances of interaction could be useful to further refine the quality of human-robotic interaction ... a robot that understands that there is a problem in the interaction by correctly interpreting the user's social signals, could let the user know that it understands the problem and actively apply error recovery strategies.'

Don't be afraid to step into the dark from time to time, and make mistakes, or at the very least create incongruencies. Many brand taglines, logos and headlines have grammatical errors in them, from McDonald's 'I'm lovin' it' to KFC's 'Finger lickin' good'. And many of the classic images in advertising don't make sense, from a meerkat in a dressing gown to a gorilla banging the drums.

The brain loves a visual puzzle or incongruity, or identifying when something is not quite right. We are wired to notice if something is out of place or doesn't quite fit thanks to the evolution of the attention system of the human brain. Marketers can take advantage of this information by deliberately making mistakes. If your ad is messy or incomplete, a consumer will spend more time processing the information or messaging. You can, in being messy, direct a consumer's attention to spend more time with a brand. Have you spent more time than you should detecting differences in two near-identical pictures? It's the same principle. We enjoy identifying and rectifying mistakes. Global eyewear brand Specsavers employed this strategy in their 'Specsavers spot the mistakes' advertisement. The ad featured a man renovating his daughter's cubby house, only to realise that he had renovated the family dog's kennel. There were 15 mistakes embedded in the ad, with viewers invited to spot the errors and go in the running for a weekly $1000 prize.

Minor mistakes in a product can increase its desirability and intent to purchase. In behavioural economics, this is referred to as 'blemishing'.[51] Research suggests desirability for a brand increases when the brand is presented as slightly imperfect. This included wine glasses, hiking books and chocolate. The same principle applies to restaurant reviews. People are more attracted to a restaurant if there's a hurdle, such as terrible parking, because they believe the restaurant must be fantastic to overcome these negatives. In addition, references to the difficulties of parking make the reviews appear more authentic. Here are two examples of the blemishing principle in action.

There are twigs in Monteith's cider

Monteith's is a New Zealand brewing company that wanted buyers to know its cider is made with fresh fruit. How did they quickly establish their credentials? They shoved some twigs into the packaging of their crushed apple cider and crushed pear cider. After several people contacted the company, it issued an 'apology' saying the twigs are a by-product of making cider with fresh fruit. Consumers were welcome to use other brands made from concentrate, with no twigs in sight. The promotional twig campaign saw sales increase by 32 per cent.

The labels won't stick

In the year 2000, Howard Cearns, Nic Trimboli and Phil Sexton founded the brewery Little Creatures, creating a wonderful award-winning beer. Over long, hot summer days, I'd store Little Creatures beers in an esky. After a while, the label would start to peel away from the bottle. By the end of the day, most of the labels would be off completely, and you were left drinking beer from a plain brown bottle. This was a known issue for the brand, with many people complaining about it. Nothing was done about the labels for many years.

When I asked Howard about the slippery labels, I expected him to tell me it was a deliberate ploy to give a unique, hand-crafted feel to the beer. The real reason was slightly different. Howard said,

The bottles had to be sourced in small parcels from places like Portugal because Australian manufacturers only did large-scale runs and Fosters wasn't going to allow us to use the VB bottle any time soon. The imported bottles had difficult surfaces requiring unique change parts. There was too much moisture as they came through the new labeller, causing havoc. You are forgiven for a while, but then you have to make them stick.

This imperfection was because of a scrappy, resourceful approach. The non-sticking labels, although a fault, became a signifier of a better-quality beer. Howard then spoke about his latest venture, craft vodka. 'We recently bottled our first batch of craft vodka out of the Hippocampus Distillery and guess what? The neck labels don't stick properly. You have to smile.' And smile he will, because again the imperfect labels will signify a more bespoke product.

Little Creatures has since been bought out by Lion Nathan and it has fixed the issues with the labels. They won't peel off if left in an esky of melting ice all day. And in fixing the labels, they've arguably compromised the authenticity of the brand a little.

4. Make a mess

Think of the best online brands in the world, and now think of their user experience. I think Facebook has one of the worst user experiences. Not only that, but the company continually changes its rules and users have to adjust. I'm not sure if this is deliberate, but it doesn't feel particularly consumer-obsessed or consumer-focused. And yet the brand is successful. If consumers say they want a seamless experience with your brand, don't believe them. Or better yet, believe them, but don't give them what they say they want. Instead, hunt for opportunities to cause confusion, make mistakes or be wasteful.

The flip side of fluency

When I was in New York for business, I met with Adam Alter, a very smooth and free-flowing young chap. He's an associate professor of Marketing at the Stern School of Business, which is a part of New York University. Adam's book *Drunk Tank Pink* was a *New York Times* bestseller and an exploratory book on the power of behavioural economics. Like me, he has a background in marketing and psychology and has effortlessly (it seems) become an opinion leader in the world of 'fluency'. Adam became interested in the topic of cognitive fluency when studying for his PhD with supervisor, Danny Oppenheimer. I reference Danny in my book *The Advertising Effect: How to change behaviour.*

Adam rose to global prominence when interviewed for an article in the *Boston Globe* titled 'Easy = True: How cognitive fluency shapes what we believe, how we invest, and who will become a supermodel'. I highly recommend the article and Adam's book.

Adam describes the concept of cognitive fluency as

the ease or difficulty you experience when making sense of a piece of information. For example, this sentence is fluent: 'The cat sat on the mat.' And this one means the same thing, but is more disfluent, or difficult to process: 'The mat was sat on by the cat.' You can manipulate fluency by choosing clear (fluent) or ornate (disfluent) fonts, by adjusting the contrast between the foreground and background in an image or piece of text, by choosing long or short words and using many other approaches.

People prefer fluency to disfluency; some of Adam's work has even shown that having a fluent name helps lawyers 'become partners at law firms more quickly' than lawyers whose names are disfluent, and that stocks starting out on the market do better if they have simple names. I think the name 'Adam Alter' has a high degree of fluency, and he is a well-known thinker on the subject. (I didn't ask him if he might not be as famous if his name didn't have alliteration for fear of being a bit of a shit.)

Cognitive fluency is related to many ideas described in behavioural economics. It's perhaps best explained using Daniel Kahneman's System 1 and System 2 thinking, discussed in chapter 3.

German radiologist Christine Born examined what happened in people's brains when they looked at various brands while in an MRI machine. The study revealed brains respond better to strong brands.

The results showed that strong brands activated a network of cortical areas and areas involved in positive emotional processing and associated with self-identification and rewards. The activation pattern was independent of the category of the product or the service being offered. Furthermore, strong brands were processed with less effort on the part of the brain. Weak brands showed higher levels of activation in areas of working memory and negative emotional response.[52]

So, all good. Create a sense of cognitive fluency and people will choose your brand over another. But what if your competitors are already doing this? How do you stop or interrupt the cognitive flow and get people to consider your brand next to your most established competition?

As Adam puts it, the power of disfluency can be summed up in this way:

People spend only as much mental energy as they need (and no more) to reach an adequate solution. You can encourage people to spend more energy by making the task seem more complicated or by making them feel less confident in their responses. One way to do this is to make the experience more disfluent. For example, if you print a question in a font that's hard to read, it seems harder to answer, even though the question itself hasn't changed. There's some evidence that people spend more time and energy solving problems that are printed in the harder-to-read font.

Creating disfluent brand experiences means more extended processing, so people sit with them for longer. Adam mentioned a study from the

University of Michigan.[53] They asked people this seemingly simple question: 'How many animals of each kind did Moses take on the Ark? Most people answer with 'two'. But it was Noah, not Moses, who was on the Ark. However, it was easier to say 'two' rather than stop and pay attention to every word in the question. Our brains take a few words and fill in the blanks for us. We're not expecting to see an error in the question, so we ignore it. We create cognitive fluency. This is excellent news for brand Moses but not for brand Noah.

Yet the researchers found that people would question the statement a little more if it was written in an ugly and difficult-to-read font. In this instance, there was a low level of processing fluency and this, as predicted, led to more people detecting the misleading nature of the question, and identifying the correct answer as 'zero'. In making people use more effort to process the information, Noah is recognised as the mastermind. Participants were less likely to rely on spontaneous association when the font was difficult to read. If you want people to pay attention and break 'cognitive fluency' flow, make your audience work a little harder. If your brand isn't number one in a category, remember this. Make people think or they may not think of you.

In marketing, the category leader will (almost by definition) be the brand that most benefits from any misattribution. Whenever anyone advertises in a particular category, people may remember the ad but incorrectly attribute it to a brand that wasn't advertising. The market leader invariably has more customer loyalty, higher penetration and more overall users, so more people associate anything to do with the category with that particular brand.

Brands that aren't the market leader — challenger brands — have to be noticed and cut through. These brands also have to ensure that anything the brand does is attributed to that brand. A possible solution to this problem is cognitive disfluency. Make people work harder to process information about your brand. They'll code it more deeply, remember it for longer and realise it was you and not the competitor talking to them.

But Adam cautions about making people work too hard, recommending disfluency be used sparingly and judiciously; if a message is too difficult to decode, people will just disengage.

Don't forget this

My previous agency, Naked Communications, did very well at the 2019 Cannes Lions, the pinnacle of advertising creativity. There was a lot of interest in its project with RMIT University that created a new font to help students retain important information. Called 'Sans Forgetica', the font was constructed using the principle of 'desirable difficulty'. The font is harder to process than other fonts because bits of each letter are missing. This additional layer of difficulty means readers have to work harder to process the font and, as a result, their memory of the content improves. The font has been downloaded more than 300 000 times, and the team at RMIT believes it could help in learning languages and for those with Alzheimer's disease.[54]

This chapter has loads of mistakes in it, as does the rest of book, I'm sure. I did it as a deliberate ploy so you would remember my favourite marketing tactics designed to get consumers to see and stick with your brand.

chapter 12
ask what your consumer can do for you

One of the reasons I'm cynical about market research and insight is it projects forwards and attempts to guess and anticipate how people will act. People are more likely to rationalise their actions after the fact than act rationally. We are terrible historians of our own behaviour and even worse predictors of it. The human condition is to act first, think later.

Attitude follows action

When I worked at the prison, my supervisor often talked about our chances of survival if we weren't junior psychologists but inmates locked up and made to tough it out with the other inmates. To my surprise, my supervisor said I would cope very well. His rationale was that I was good at getting people to do things for me. There would be many inmates who would look after me, because they'd invested in me. This chapter explores my favourite theme from my previous book, *The Advertising Effect: How to change behaviour*. It's that 'action changes attitude faster than attitude changes action'. If you want people to like you, ask them to do something for you. For your business or personal life, this is very useful.

One of the counterintuitive concepts I've come across in marketing is this: ask not what you can do for your customers, but what your customers can do for you. It is related to the psychological theory of cognitive dissonance that states we feel uncomfortable if our thoughts, feelings and actions are not aligned. We make them align by changing the thinking, feeling or action. When you ask someone to do you a small favour, they're more likely to view you positively as a consequence of that action. In a marketing sense, the more a consumer interacts with your brand, the more wedded they become to the brand.

How do you feel when buying something for the first time? You may feel intrigued or unsure about a brand. Or you may feel neutral and grab it absentmindedly. If your preferred brand wasn't available on the shelf, you might have felt mild hesitation. How do you feel post purchase? You've just invested several dollars and time and effort towards that brand. If you've bought the brand for someone else, the kids, for example, then you have to spend time convincing them that the brand is good. These processes make you feel positive about the brand. And this is why businesses invest in trials and product samples. (But I should note, cognitive dissonance may not be enough to overcome a poor product experience.)

It's also the reason so much brand tracking is silly. We don't move from awareness to interest to desire to action. It's more likely we move from awareness to action to interest and desire. That is, 'action changes attitude faster than attitude changes action' and if we're able to get people to act, then they'll be more likely to reward us with continued interest. Ever wondered why people seeking donations for charities often ask an innocuous opening question? If you answer, you're involved. And once you're involved, you're more likely to donate. This is the reason brands such as Aesop have free samples.

The Aesop effect

Personal care brand Aesop is a great Australian success story. No doubt you've seen the brand's liquid soap proudly sitting in many bathrooms. Established in Melbourne in 1987 and named after an ancient Greek storyteller, many of its products feature a line of poetry. Founder Dennis Paphitis and creative director Suzanne Santos conceived Aesop's vision.

For many years my good friend Saurenne was Dennis's executive assistant. Dennis is exacting, with very clear ideas about what Aesop stands for, and this philosophy runs through the organisation. At the head office (which is never seen by customers) the use of blue pens is banned. Everyone has to write with a black pen because Dennis thinks black ink is neater. There is also a clean desk policy, and before employees go home, their desk has to be cleared entirely.

Each store's design reflects the brand's values. When you enter an Aesop store, you are transported into a cocoon of design, care and beauty. Each store has a distinctive look that reflects its location. A traditionally upmarket part of town may have a store with padded dark leather on the walls. But if you walk a few kilometres to the grungy, artsy part of the city, the store might feature plywood boxes with autumn leaves scattered on the ground. A store in Montreal has three birch trees in the middle of its floor. Retail staff are trained to deliver on this casually elegant feel and connect with customers at a deeper level than other retailers. Dennis banned the team from talking about the weather because he said the weather is already evident.

Aesop is a classic case of a company that conducts its marketing from the inside out led by a founder and CEO who behaves as the chief brand officer. Dennis' insistence that staff only use black pens seems like a small thing, but it means Aesop employees need to make sense of this exacting behaviour. They do this by aligning their thoughts with their actions to avoid cognitive dissonance. Staff might rationalise that the insistence they only write in black is weird, but because they believe in the brand and want it to grow, they agree to the request. The same logic applies to conversation topics with customers. The idea of coming up with interesting discussion points to engage customers scares the hell out of me. But in making staff creative with their conversation starters, Dennis forces them to put effort into the Aesop brand — making them wedded to the brand.

The company has nailed critical touchpoints and is globally success- ful. But in my view, Aesop's best strategy is its unrelenting supply of samples. Since the company's inception, Dennis insists that customers be able to sample the products. If you walk past an Aesop store, there are pump packs of moisturiser that passers-by can sample. At any Aesop store, you can take a handful of sachet samples with you. Saurenne always had plenty of sachets to hand out to her friends. Samples would be available at poetry readings, book launches and select conferences. Dennis didn't worry that the samples would cannibalise a sale. He was convinced that once people have tried the product, they'd love it and make a purchase.

Even though the samples are perceived as a gift, all it does is encourage people to rip the pack open and try it on their skin. When it's on their skin, they feel more positive about it. In psychology, this is called 'the endowment effect', which states we are more likely to value brands and objects if we hold them or 'own' them in some way. In the case of Aesop products, once you feel it on your skin, you like it more. It's the same reason that retailers want you to remove a dress from the rack and hold it. You value it more if you hold it. The endowment effect can even be observed in online shopping if there's a touch screen.[55]

It's also worth mentioning that Aesop has never spent a dollar on advertising. Through the samples, distinctive store design, media coverage and select sponsorships of events, the Aesop brand has grown across the globe. He may not have heard of cognitive dissonance, but Dennis has achieved a customer base that thinks, feels and acts positively towards his brand. Customers have invested in his brand through their actions, which helped to build the brand. He did it beautifully.

space

My friend CJ Holden describes himself as an 'experientialist'. After working at a rebel trade event known as LE Miami, which I spoke at, he asked for my advice about moving to Australia. I said, 'Why don't you just create an event?' We'd had ongoing conversations about the stiff and predictable nature of most corporate conferences, with delegates stuck in row after row of chairs for a day or two listening to 40-minute chunks of content. The only opportunity to meet other attendees is during morning tea and lunch. And if you wanted to meet the speakers, forget about it. Most speakers fly in and fly out and rarely stay for the entire conference. We wanted to change this approach and decided to stage a conference together. CJ had one requirement. It had to be unlike any conference we'd ever been to. By bringing people together to create a new kind of experience, we would 'ask something of the customer' and construct a community of people to co-create the brand and be the experience.

When CJ sent me a business plan, at the top of the document was the phrase: 'Watch This Space'. I thought this was his name for the conference and loved it. He said 'Adam, that's not the name. I don't have a name yet'. A few days later, he suggested we call it 's p a c e' because it's neater and more prominent. He was right, and s p a c e was born. We invited Holly Ransom to be part of the conference because she's one of Australia's most successful young business leaders. (To illustrate her credentials, when US President Barack Obama gave an exclusive talk in Sydney, he was in conversation with Holly.)

To make s p a c e work we needed to attract a community of people invested in its success. We asked friends and family to suggest interesting people who might want to help us develop the concept. There were many workshops with pizza and wine as we worked to build the idea. These people gave their time, effort and expertise to the cause, which meant they felt invested in the success of s p a c e.

This conference didn't separate speakers and delegates. There were no official speakers. Every attendee was a delegate and speaker. And everyone was expected to stay the whole time (three nights and two days — not three days and two nights). Attendees had to contribute to the 'conference' (and I'm calling it a conference, but it was more festival than a conference). Each delegate received a s p a c e pack that asked whether they would contribute a talk, video, adventure or another idea of their devising. People were excited about what they would create. CJ spoke with each of the 240 delegates to ensure they were happy about their contribution. As CJ described in an interview with *Echo* newspaper,

You choose your own adventure. We remove titles, places of work. Every single session you go to you don't know who's running it — you will turn up because of the power of the title. Anyone can apply. This

is not a CEO retreat. It's not a marketing or advertising conference. It's not innovation. It's about finding people who are passionate about Australia and want to be a force for change.[2]

On the first night, the rain bucketed down. We held a dinner and fireside chat with two of the more well-known delegates, one famous and one infamous. They were Jules Lund, TV presenter turned technology entrepreneur and founder of social influencer company TRIBE. He interviewed the recently notorious 'egg boy', 17-year-old Will Connolly, who'd thrown an egg at then-Senator Fraser Anning. Jules and Will set the scene for a rather special event.

The action started the following morning. Ten large boards were placed next to each other and divided into different parts of the day. Everyone wrote their session on a card. After a somewhat chaotic hour, we had ten boards filled with 240 sessions spread over the full two days that people could go and see.

It felt magical as everyone wandered around, creating their conference from the content on display. Some sessions only had three or four people in them, while others had a hundred or so. A massive gong sounded when it was time to move to the next session. With so much on offer, you had to plan your time carefully. In case things went awry, a 's p a c e' facilitator was in each session, but nothing went wrong. When it was time for a delegate to become the leader, they did so. It was an exciting experience.

Over the next two days, people wove in and out of various sessions on a range of topics including how to self-brand, men experiencing what it's like to cry, treasure hunts and discussions about making a meaningful life without kids. There were conversations about films, how businesses can break into China, and how to manage troublesome employees. Each session fulfilled s p a c e's core mission of creating a more ambitious Australia. It did this by facilitating unexpected conversations between unlikely people. It was a massive success. Our post-conference satisfaction scores were through the roof and created substantial buzz.

I'm sure part of its success relates to the power of cognitive dissonance. Everyone who attended had to contribute and co-build the event, so everyone who spoke or contributed (which was everyone) now has a vested interest in s p a c e. They are part of a community that will help it grow into the future. There were no passive attendees. Everyone who attended spent several hours of preparation thinking about the conference, and during the conference put effort into co-creating it. Exerting this effort meant they were more inclined to enjoy it. Between you and me, I do wonder if delegates agree with this assessment. I hope so.

Doing nothing does harm

Since starting Thinkerbell, one of the campaigns I'm most proud of is 'Doing Nothing Does Harm'. It was created for Our Watch, an organisation that addresses violence against women and children by changing culture and behaviours. It's focused on the prevention of abuse and changing behaviours that make violence more likely. We wanted to address bystander behaviour where people don't call out sexism. You might witness sexism but dismiss it as harmless.

With the insight that 'action changes attitude faster than attitude changes action', we decided to create a series of ads that allowed online interaction. When there was a sexist comment, a button appeared on the ad that read, 'To stop this sexist behaviour, click here', next to a five-second counter. Those that clicked the button saw an alternative ending to the video where a bystander takes action and calls out the sexist comment. They also received a message rewarding them for their pro-social behaviour. It read: THANKS FOR DOING SOMETHING TO STOP SEXIST BEHAVIOUR. YOU WON'T SEE THESE ADS AGAIN. It empowered those who intervened and rewarded them. We 'de-targeted' rather than 're-targeted' viewers. It was a world first.

By contrast, those who didn't 'intervene' continued to be targeted and the sexist behaviour became progressively worse. Counter messages dramatising the implications of not acting also appeared including: TO SEE MORE DISRESPECT TOWARDS WOMEN, KEEP DOING NOTHING. The campaign gave viewers the tools to take action, helped them practise pro-social behaviour and rewarded them. The hope is they'll take these skills into the real world and speak up if they witness sexism.

It's challenging to measure the impact of the campaign, but we used benchmarks that asked people if they knew how to intervene when witnessing sexist behaviour. After watching and interacting with the campaign, these metrics increased. The campaign achieved extensive reach and earned media. Even though sexist attitudes are fairly entrenched, this campaign showed that an ability to practise online is positive. I think interactive campaigns will become more prevalent.

So will you do something for me?

When you finish reading this book, which is really soon, can you do me a favour and visit Twitter or Instagram and use the hashtag #Stoplisteningtothecustomer? It's much appreciated. This reminds me of the old car bumper stickers that read, 'Honk if you listen to X radio station'. I'm surprised a commercial radio station hasn't revived that sticker in a retro promotion.

chapter 13
the closing argument

So I think that just about does it. As a recap, this book set out to explain the reasons why listening to the customer can be at the expense of growing a brand. Throughout my life, I've been fascinated by the power of marketing and branding. I'm amazed at how marketing and advertising can encourage us to make completely illogical decisions, such as buying a product that's twice as expensive as a near-identical one. Creating brands is complicated and sensitive. There needs to be clarity in how the brand is established and consistency in taking it to market. This balance of clarity and consistency needs to be derived from the brand itself, not the consumer.

Marketing and branding have a terrible reputation. The publisher of this book, John Wiley & Sons, is branding it as a business book because marketing books don't sell. I think this sullied reputation is contributing to marketers looking in all the wrong places to justify their marketing decisions. These include consumer research and consumer insight, rather than marketing and branding strategy, with marketing sciences.

Hopefully I've made a compelling argument that listening to the consumer will ultimately destroy your brand. This is because fundamentally, consumers don't need your brand or product. If it exists in an established category, there is at least one alternative to satisfy the consumer. Listening to the customer makes you smaller. You'll stay out of the consumer's way and meet generic category needs because that's what they want.

The alternative to listening to the customer is developing brand intelligence and prioritising what your brand stands for beyond everything else. The ultimate in brand intelligence is to create a brand so motivating and differentiated that it busts through preconceptions and creates a category of one. My friend Rob Perkin's feel-good business 'OMGyes' is a brilliant example. But this approach isn't always possible or always needed.

Brand growth within a category is possible and, as outlined in the book, stands the best chance of success if the organisation is aligned around the brand and what it stands for. For brands to grow, they need to create mental and physical availability — which is most comfortable if everyone is clear on what the brand stands for. From the board to the CEO (I mean chief brand officer), the CMO and across the organisation, if all are behind the brand, decisions are faster and brands can act tactically and enjoy increased earned media. An example is our work with the iconic brand Vegemite. The 'Tastes Like Australia' platform has liberated the brand, allowing it to act with tactical, attention-getting freedom.

Next up are brands doing what I can't imagine many consumers recommending, and that's to embrace their dark side and shine a light on their negatives and weaknesses. In a world chasing perfection and efficiency, powered by ridiculous insights supplied by human-centred designers, creating friction, and getting people to stop and think is to be applauded. We'll have to work harder to generate friction, create waste, make mistakes and make a mess. But it's worth it because people will spend more time processing brands and messages.

And failing that, stop doing things for the customer and instead get your customer to do things for you. Invite them to co-create your products like IKEA, or, at the very least, ask them to be involved in the marketing by investing part of themselves into the brand. The more you ask them to be involved, the more they'll like you. To read more about this, grab of copy of my previous book, *The Advertising Effect: How to change behaviour.*

It's challenging to create the new, the unusual, the attention-getting and the different. The more people we ask, the more we are drawn to the middle ground of mediocrity. As an individual, it's hard to stand your ground and believe in yourself. However, a brand needs to convince an entire organisation to stay the course — and it can be diverted very quickly. Listening to consumers increases the risk of homogenisation and brand devaluation. Stop listening to your customers and try hearing your brand instead.

appendix:
the 'how cool are you' questionnaire

Answer the following questions as accurately as you can. Try and go with your first impression and don't overthink each question. Answers range from Strongly Disagree (1) to Strongly Agree (5), with Neutral in the middle (3). Please try and use the full spectrum of 1 to 5 in your answers.

	QUESTION	SD SA
1	I often feel invisible in social situations.	1 2 3 4 5
2	I have a strong sense of who I am and what I stand for.	1 2 3 4 5
3	It's more important to act in a manner true to your character than it is to keep others happy.	1 2 3 4 5
4	I'm not easily influenced by others' opinions.	1 2 3 4 5
5	I like to keep up with what's on trend.	1 2 3 4 5
6	I'm often described as a real individual.	1 2 3 4 5
7	My career is my passion.	1 2 3 4 5
8	I don't tend to fit in.	1 2 3 4 5
9	I'm very feminine.	1 2 3 4 5

(continued)

	QUESTION	SD SA
10	I don't like to talk about the things I've achieved.	1 2 3 4 5
11	I tend to keep my emotions under control.	1 2 3 4 5
12	People say I'm pretty understated, even when things go my way.	1 2 3 4 5
13	I'm sometimes selfish and rude more than I need to be.	1 2 3 4 5
14	People say I'm sensitive to the needs of others.	1 2 3 4 5
15	I'm in a career (or volunteer position) where I care for others.	1 2 3 4 5
16	It's more important to share wealth than it is to be wealthy.	1 2 3 4 5
17	I'm a couch potato and while away days being a recluse.	1 2 3 4 5
18	I tend to attract people to me.	1 2 3 4 5
19	I'm pretty sociable.	1 2 3 4 5
20	People think I'm pretty influential.	1 2 3 4 5
TOTAL		

To mark your cool questionnaire you'll simply add up all the numbers you've circled and that will give you a total number out of 100. However, before you add the numbers please reverse your score for questions numbered 1, 5, 9, 13 and 17. That is if you scored a 5 on these questions please give yourself a 1, if you scored a 4 please give yourself a 2, and if you scored a 3 then just leave it as it is. Now add up all your scores for all 20 questions and find out your cool quotient of 100.

COOL QUOTIENT	COOL PROFILE
96–100: Ice Ice Baby: You're so damn cool that you don't need a questionnaire to tell you what you already know. Well done. **76–95:** Cool Cat: You're very cool and people around you are glad to have someone so cool hanging out with them. However, don't rest on your laurels. You've still got work to do if you want to be cooler. **60–75:** Luke Warm Cool: Okay well at least you're not 'normal'. You've got some cool tendencies you can work on. Focus on these, work hard and you too could become cool. **50–60:** Dick and Jane: Don't worry about trying to be cool, rejoice in being normal. It's much easier than being cool, not as rewarding, but easier! **Under 50:** Overstated Underachiever? Not sure what you've done to score so low. Life may be a little tough for you in our cool obsessed world!	Please note that your questionnaire reveals what factors you need to work harder at to be cool. Questions 1 to 4 reveal your 'Self-Belief and Confidence' score, out of 20. Questions 5 to 8 reveal your 'Defying Convention' score, out of 20. Questions 9 to 12 reveal your 'Understated Achievement' score, out of 20. Questions 13 to 16 reveal your 'Caring For Others' score, out of 20, and Questions 17 to 20 reveal your 'Connectivity and Influence' score, out of 20.

about the authors

Adam Ferrier

Founder, Thinkerbell / s p a c e / MSIX

Adam Ferrier is a multi-award-winning advertising creative and founder of the agency Thinkerbell. He is a leading Australian consumer psychologist and top creative strategist. Adam obtained degrees in Commerce and Clinical Psychology before beginning his career in Forensic Psychology. He then switched his focus from criminal behaviour to consumer behaviour and joined marketing consultancy Added Value. Adam went on to become a Founding Partner of Naked Communications APAC before co-founding Thinkerbell in 2017. Thinkerbell has gone on to become Adnews Creative Agency of the Year, and Mumbrella Agency of the year (2019), and works with many of Australia's top brands. Adam sits on the boards of social influencing company TRIBE, as well as The Public Interest Journalism Initiative (PIJI). Further, Adam is a weekly guest on national breakfast show Sunrise, and regular media commentator. His first book *The Advertising Effect: How to change behaviour* was published in 2014. Adam is also a renowned keynote speaker with ODE management.

Jen Fleming

Jen Fleming is an acclaimed producer, reporter and presenter. She's worked with Australia's best-known presenters at ABC Radio Sydney and currently produces Afternoons with James Valentine. Jen has co-written several books including the best-selling *Spotless* series, *The Feel Good Body*, *The Australian Healthy Hormone Diet* and Adam's previous book, *The Advertising Effect: How to change behaviour.*

endnotes

1 Kantar (2019). 'Brandz top 100 most valuable global brands 2019'. http://online.pubhtml5.com/bydd/ksdy/#p=18

2 Baxter, M. (2018). 'Think Different. Yeah, not so much'. LinkedIn. https://www.linkedin.com/pulse/why-you-should-sell-your-apple-shares-mat-baxter/

3 Zealley, J. (2019). 'Meet the new brand of CMO'. Accenture Interactive. https://www.accenture.com/ca-en/insights/consulting/cmo

4 ibid.

5 From his poem 'La Pucelle d'Orléans' (The Maid of Orleans), which is a satire on Joan of Arc.

6 Svenson, O. (1981). 'Are we all less risky and more skillful than our fellow drivers?'. *Acta Psychologica*, 47 (2): 143–148.

7 Upamanyu, N.U., Mathur, G., & Bhakar, S.S. (2014). 'The connection between self-concept (actual self congruence & ideal self congruence) on brand preferences'. *International Journal of Management Excellence*, vol. 3, no. 1.

8 Morwitz, V.J., Steckel, J.H., & Gupta, A. (2007). 'When do purchase intentions predict sales?'. *International Journal of Forecasting*, vol. 23, iss. 3, pp. 347–364.

9 https://marketingland.com/wp-content/ml-loads/2018/01/ Engagement-on-Facebook-When-it-Matters_3.10.14.pdf

10 Danziger, S., Levav, J., & Avnaim-Pesso, L. (2011). 'Extraneous factors in judicial decisions'. *PNAS* April 26, vol. 108, iss. 17.

11 Ambler, T. (2005). 'The waste in advertising is the part that works'. *Journal of Advertising Research*, vol. 44, iss. 4.

12 Sharp, B. (2012). *How Brands Grow: What marketers don't know*. Oxford University Press.

13 Snijders, W. (2018). 'The unbearable lightness of buying, as told by an old jar of pesto'. Mumbrella. https://mumbrella. com.au/the-unbearable-lightness-of-buying-as-told-by-an-old-jar-of-pesto-550525

14 Heath, R. (2012). *Seducing the subconscious*. Wiley.

15 Piacenza, J. (2017). 'U.S. adults warming to Twitter's 280-character expansion'. Morning Consult. https:// morningconsult.com/2017/10/13/u-s-adults-likely-favor-twitters-280-character-expansion/

16 Rosen, A. (2017). 'Tweeting made easier'. Twitter blog. https://blog.twitter.com/en_us/topics/product/2017/ tweetingmadeeasier.html

17 Oremus, W. (2018). 'Remember when longer tweets were the thing that was going to kill Twitter?'. Slate. https://slate.com/ technology/2018/10/twitter-tweet-character-limits-280-140-effect.html

18 McIntyre, P. (2019). 'IAG CMO Brent Smart: martech is "hygiene", everyone's doing it, no competitive advantage'. Mi3. https://www.mi-3.com.au/15-07-2019/iag-cmo-brent-smart-martech-hygiene-everyones-doing-it-and-theres-no-competitive

19 Creswell, J. (2018). 'How Amazon steers shoppers to its own products'. *The New York Times*. https://www.nytimes. com/2018/06/23/business/amazon-the-brand-buster.html

20 Alexander, V. (2019). 'I've been designing offices for decades. Here's what I got wrong'. *Fast Company*. https://www.

fastcompany.com/90373440/ive-been-designing-offices-for-decades-heres-what-i-got-wrong

21 Pattisall, J. (2019). *The Cost of Losing Creativity: The ROI model for agency creativity.* Forrester.

22 Hanft, A. (2015). 'The Zombie-mobile'. Medium.

23 Slater, S., & Narver, J.C. (1996). 'Customer-led and market-oriented: Let's not confuse the two'. *Strategic Management Journal*, vol. 19, iss. 10, pp. 1001–1006.

24 Inzlicht, M., Shenhav, A., & Olivola C.Y. (2018). 'The Effort Paradox: Effort is both costly and valued'. *Trends in Cognitive Science*, vol.22, iss. 4, pp. 337–349.

25 Sandra, D., & Otto, A.R. (2018) 'Cognitive capacity limitations and need for cognition differentially predict reward-induced cognitive effort expenditure'. *Cognition* iss. 172, 101–106.

26 Norton M.I. et al., (2012). 'The IKEA effect: when labor leads to love'. *Journal of Consumer Psychology*, iss. 22, pp. 453–460.

27 The results are discussed by Professor Mark Ritson as part of the Gold Effie wrap up. https://www.youtube.com/watch?v=ZHgfp83k-10.

28 You can see the two ads at http://www.tourism.australia.com/en/about/our-campaigns/dundee.html.

29 Leberecht, T. (2015). *The Business Romantic.* HarperBusiness.

30 ALDI Unpacked. 'Behind the scenes of what makes ALDI Good different'. https://www.aldiunpacked.com.au/Article/August-2018/Behind-the-scenes-of-what-makes-ALDI-Good-Differen

31 Isaac, M. (2019). 'How Uber got lost'. *The New York Times*. https://www.nytimes.com/2019/08/23/business/how-uber-got-lost.html

32 Ritson, M. (2018). 'Byron Sharp is wrong — of course brand perceptions influence sales'. MarketingWeek. https://www.marketingweek.com/mark-ritson-byron-sharp-brand-perceptions/

33 Raymundo, O. 'Richard Branson on the secret to building an exceptional company'. *Inc.* https://www.inc.com/oscar-raymundo/richard-branson-secret-of-exceptional-companies.html

34 Evans, S. (2018). 'Cabcharge jumps 30pc as Uber surge-pricing disappoints'. *Australian Financial Review.* https://www.afr.com/business/transport/automobile/cabcharge-jumps-30-per-cent-as-uber-surge-pricing-disappoints-20180612-h1195p

35 Arkwright, D. (2014). 'Dirt is good: how storytelling gave Persil a boost'. Campaign. https://www.campaignlive.co.uk/article/dirt-good-storytelling-gave-persil-boost/1287039

36 From the website 'Diamonds in the Lines'

37 Hart, D.L. (1977). 'The classical Jungian school' in Young-Eisendrath, P., & Dawson, T. *The Cambridge Companion to Jung.* Cambridge, p. 92.

38 Adler, J.M., & Olin, F.W. (2012). 'Living Into the Story: Agency and coherence in a longitudinal study of narrative identity development and mental health over the course of psychotherapy'. *Journal of Personality and Social Psychology,* vol. 102, iss. 2, pp. 367–389.

39 Bosman, M. (2012). 'You Might Not Like it, But Bad is Stronger than Good'.

40 Baumeister, R.F., & Bratslavsky, E. (2001). 'Bad is stronger than good'. *Review of General Psychology,* vol. 5., iss. 4., pp. 323–370

41 Cacioppo, J.T. et al. (2009). 'In the Eye of the Beholder: individual differences in perceived social isolation predict regional brain activation to social stimuli'. *Journal of Cognitive Neuroscience,* vol. 21, iss. 1, pp. 83–92.

42 Trussler, M., & Soroka, S. (2014). 'Consumer demand for cynical and negative news frames'. *The International Journal of Press and Politics,* vol. 19, iss. 3, pp. 360–379.

43 Crick, P. (2017). 'Negative superlatives in headlines?'. cre8ive Marketing. https://cre8ive.co.nz/superlatives-headlines/

44 Cheung, E.O., & Gardner, W.L. (2015). 'The way I make you feel: Social exclusion enhances the ability to manage others' emotions'. *Journal of Experimental Social Psychology*, iss. 60, pp. 59–75

45 Australian Institute of Health and Welfare, web report. (2019). 'Deaths in Australia'. https://www.aihw.gov.au/reports/life-expectancy-death/deaths-in-australia/contents/leading-causes-of-death

46 Tracksafe Foundation NZ. (2016). 'The conscious crossing'. https://www.youtube.com/watch?v=T_DZPdOhjNM

47 Syme, G. et al. (2000). 'The evaluation of information campaigns to promote voluntary household water conservation'. *Evaluation Review*, vol. 24, pp. 539–578; Smart Water Fund. (2006). 'Development and trial of smart shower meter demonstration prototypes'. Project Smart1. InvetechPty Ltd.

48 Van Der Linden, S. (2011). 'How the illusion of being observed can make you a better person'. *Scientific American*. http://www.bbc.com/future/story/20140209-being-watched-why-thats-good

49 Ambler, T., & Hollier, E.A. (2004). 'The waste in advertising is the part that works'. *Journal of Advertising Research*, vol. 44, iss. 4, pp. 375–389.

50 Buell, R.W., & Norton, M.I. (2011). 'The labor illusion: how operational transparency increases perceived value'. *Management Science*, vol. 57, iss. 9, pp. 1564–1579.

51 Shiv, B., Danit, E., & Zakary, L.T. (2012). 'When blemishing leads to blossoming: the positive effect of negative information'. *Journal of Consumer Research*, vol. 38, iss. 5.

52 ScienceDaily. (2006). 'MRI shows brains respond better to name brands'. Radiological Society of North America. https://www.sciencedaily.com/releases/2006/11/061128083022.htm

53 Song, H., & Schwarz, N. (2008). 'Fluency and the detection of misleading questions: low processing fluency attenuates the Moses Illusion'. *Social Cognition*, vol. 26, pp. 791–799.

54 RMIT University. (2018). 'Sans Forgetica. The font to remember'. https://www.rmit.edu.au/media-objects/multimedia/video/eve/marketing/sans-forgetica-the-font-to-remember

55 Brasel, A., & Gips, J. (2014). 'Tablets, touchscreens, and touchpads: how varying touch interfaces trigger psychological ownership and endowment'. *Journal of Consumer Psychology*, vol. 24, iss. 2, pp. 226–232.

56 Nolan, M. (2019). 'Exploring s p a c e for the future!'. echo.net.au. https://www.echo.net.au/2019/04/exploring-s-p-c-e-future/

index